SYSTEMS THINKING
STRATEGY

SYSTEMS THINKING
STRATEGY

THE NEW WAY TO UNDERSTAND YOUR
BUSINESS AND DRIVE PERFORMANCE

JIMMY BROWN, PHD

iUniverse, Inc.
Bloomington

Systems Thinking Strategy
The New Way to Understand Your Business and Drive Performance

Copyright © 2012 by Jimmy Brown, PhD

All rights reserved. No part of this book may be used or reproduced by any means, graphic, electronic, or mechanical, including photocopying, recording, taping or by any information storage retrieval system without the written permission of the publisher except in the case of brief quotations embodied in critical articles and reviews.

iUniverse books may be ordered through booksellers or by contacting:

iUniverse
1663 Liberty Drive
Bloomington, IN 47403
www.iuniverse.com
1-800-Authors (1-800-288-4677)

Because of the dynamic nature of the Internet, any web addresses or links contained in this book may have changed since publication and may no longer be valid. The views expressed in this work are solely those of the author and do not necessarily reflect the views of the publisher, and the publisher hereby disclaims any responsibility for them.

Any people depicted in stock imagery provided by Thinkstock are models, and such images are being used for illustrative purposes only.

Certain stock imagery © Thinkstock.

ISBN: 978-1-4759-5769-3 (sc)
ISBN: 978-1-4759-5771-6 (hc)
ISBN: 978-1-4759-5770-9 (e)

Library of Congress Control Number: 2012920226

Printed in the United States of America

iUniverse rev. date: 11/06/2012

For Mei-Mei and Holden.
You are my motivation.

Contents

1: Introduction 1
2: What Is Strategy? 5
3: The Competitive Environment: Looking Outward 13
4: Leveraging Internal Capabilities 23
5: It's About the Customer... 31
6: Systems Thinking 37
7: Applying Capabilities in the STS 45
8: Applying Customer Information in the STS 55
9: The Competitive Environment in the STS 65
10: Making Sense in the STS 75
11: Lessons Learned 91
List of Figures 95
List of Tables 97
Research Notes 99
References 117
About the Author 123

1: Introduction

Why are some organizations more successful than others? Is it better products? Is it a superior service model? Is it some mixture of the two? Is it merely a matter of lining up the products and services to meet the needs of the marketplace at a particular time? Or did they just get lucky?

These are the questions business leaders wrestle with on a daily basis. And they're not just doing it for the fun of the debate. They are trying figure out how to make *their* organizations more successful. Many business leaders (especially those with top-tier MBAs) believe that finding the answer to these questions is a matter of strategy. Find the right strategy, and the company is bound to be successful.

But what is strategy? That is a tricky question. A Google search will yield around 855 million results. Narrowing the search term down to "strategic planning" is only a little better, with 145 million results. You can't go more than an hour watching CNBC or Fox Business without hearing someone use a derivation of the word. Claiming to be a *strategic thinker* has almost surpassed *good people skills* as the talent that too many people put on their résumés when they don't know what else to list.

Obviously there are a lot of people talking about strategy, but how many people really understand what it means? More importantly, how many know how to do it right? Most importantly, how can a business leader understand how to do it right and apply that to his or her organization?

Strategy is about finding ways to drive sustainable competitive advantage (Hamel, 1996; Porter, 1996; Worley, Hitchen, & Ross, 1996). There is plenty of agreement on that point. Where there is disagreement, however, is in the how, where, when, and why of the various approaches to strategy.

Notice that the previous paragraph used the word *approaches* and not the singular *approach*. That is not a typo. There are lots of different approaches to strategy, and plenty of debate about which approach is the best. While there will be some discussion of the major approaches later in this book, it is important to remember that despite proponents' claims, none of the established approaches is best for all organizations at all times. As a result, anytime one model is found to be inadequate for a particular scenario, someone comes along and presents a new approach. The majority of these models are fairly specific and applicable only to a finite number of situations. This has led to lots of different models for strategy, more than a little confusion, and numerous calls to come up with a better way (Collis & Montgomery, 1995; Cummings & Angwin, 2004; Mintzberg, 1994).

While it would be extreme hubris to claim that this book will address all of the existing models' shortcomings, it does provide an approach that has a wider application than many of the existing paradigms. This book codifies elements that reflect what many successful organizations are already doing. It takes a new view that answers at least some of the challenges presented by existing paradigms. It does this by applying a systems thinking lens (e.g., see Peter Senge's *The Fifth Discipline*) to current approaches and illustrating a model that allows for a fuller view of the organization and its ecosystem. Hopefully those who read this book will find something useful they can apply to their own organizations.

This book and the strategy model it presents are based upon a university-supported research study that was part of my doctoral dissertation. It was a long, arduous, and frankly painful process that required nearly a year and a half of literature review, data collection, and analysis, not to mention multiple rewrites. The final product, however, was an in-depth look at one very simple question:

- *Do organizations that take a systems thinking approach to strategy perform better than the overall market?*

The short answer is yes, they do. The long answer is a bit more complicated. The original dissertation and the summary report that was provided to the study participants are both hefty descriptions of what was done and why it was done, written in such a way as to appease the demands of an academic audience. But then again, that was the goal. The goal of this book is very different.

The goal of this book is to share the insights gained from that study in a way that is more palatable to business professionals without the superfluous prose of a dissertation. Accomplishing this goal will begin with an overview of what strategy is in chapter 2, followed by a look at the dominant strategy paradigms in chapters 3 through 5. Next is a review of systems thinking and how it applies to strategy in chapter 6. Chapter 6 also provides a very high-level review of the research study's methodology. Given the focus of this text, that section of chapter 6 does not go into very much detail, but for those who feel the need to "see the math," research notes are also provided at the end of the book.

Chapters 7 through 10 illustrate the major findings of the study and how they can be applied. Chapter 7 reviews how an understanding of organizational capabilities is applied; chapter 8 looks at how customer data is used; and chapter 9 looks at how information about the competitive environment is integrated into these efforts. Chapter 10 reviews how organizations make sense of all the data points. The last chapter attempts to summarize the overall findings and bring things to a reasonable close.

2: What Is Strategy?

The term *strategy* comes from the Greek word *strategos* and, loosely translated, means "art of the general" (Collis, 2005). The great Chinese general Sun Tzu said that the responsibility of generalship is to create situations that assure victory (Griffith, 1963). Following this line of reasoning, the case could be made that strategy is about creating situations that allow organizations to be victorious or, in other words, successful. Sounds simple enough, but achieving that goal can be quite complicated.

To be successful, an organization must be able to create some kind of sustainable competitive advantage. The leaders of that organization have to make hard choices about where to focus their efforts and commit their resources. The amalgamation of those decisions is called a strategy. The word strategy itself, however, is a noun, and as we all learned in elementary school, English nouns are things, not actions.

The term many people use to describe the action of strategy is *strategic planning*, but strategic planning is a specific task that drives toward a strategic plan document. These documents are usually in nice, fancy binders, but there is great debate about how much value they really provide. The basis for this debate is often questions about how often these plans reflect reality and whether they are truly executable. Moreover, strategic plans tend to be limited in scope and only present the tip of the iceberg in terms of what strategic activities the organization is engaging in.

There are many parts of the strategy process that develop, grow, and evolve outside of strategic planning sessions. These other efforts can have as much or more impact on the organization as the formal documents. It would be a disservice not to consider those elements in a comprehensive strategy discussion. For this reason, this discussion considers all strategy formulation activities, not just the ones that result in a pretty binder.

Regardless of how formal or informal the process is, once a strategy is formulated, it has to be implemented. Implementation can be just as challenging as the development, if not more so. Many organizations devote significant resources to ensuring that their strategies are effectively implemented. An important caveat here, however, is that even the best implementation will not lead to success unless the strategy that the implementation is driving toward is properly aligned with the organization's desired destination.

A mentor of mine once described scenarios like this as being like taking a long road trip with bad directions. No matter how good a driver you are, you're probably not going to get where you need to be. And even if you do somehow make it there, how will you know that you've arrived?

Since formulating the right strategy is a critical first step for setting the direction of an organization, this discussion will focus solely on the strategy formulation process. The implementation discussion will be left for another time.

Speaking of time, some might ask why a new model of strategic planning matters today? Why fix something that "ain't broke"? There are a couple of answers to such questions. First, while the current paradigms may not necessarily be "broke," they do have a number of shortcomings. There is no lack of calls to improve the overall effectiveness of those models. As to why this question needs to be addressed now, the simple answer is that the world has changed. The speed of business continues to accelerate, and how organizations are managed must also evolve.

Not so long ago, organizations could differentiate themselves based on the attributes of their products and/or delivered services. If a company's offerings were superior to the alternatives, customers would buy those offerings. Barriers to market entry tended to be high, which meant that it was rare for new alternatives to come into a market. These factors minimized competition and made strong strategic visions nice to have, but not a necessity.

As the economy has matured, however, the options for customers have increased and the barriers to entry have decreased. As a result, competition has amplified to the point where organizations must differentiate themselves not only on the basis of what they do, but also how they do it. Failure to differentiate can result in an organization's downfall. A prime example of this is Digital Equipment Corporation (Schein, 2003).

For those not familiar with this case, Digital Equipment Corporation (DEC) was one of the early leaders in the computer industry. Their VAX platform was the go-to mainframe for most businesses through the mid-1980s. Despite offering products than were better engineered and had more features than those of their competitors, DEC was unable to maintain their leadership position, due in large part to a misreading of the market and where their customers' needs were going. Their former

CEO, Ken Olsen, has become infamous for wondering why would anyone want a computer in their home (Schein, 2003, p. 37). While he has tried numerous times to clarify this statement so as not to seem quite so oblivious, the simple fact is that at the time, the organization did not see the market evolving, and thus did not alter their product focus to react to those changes. As a result, DEC no longer exists today.

One way that some organizations have tried to mitigate the risks of relying solely on a product-quality-based advantage has been to establish an early foothold in a market, or even to create an entirely new space. Sometimes these brands become ubiquitous within a particular product category. Such has been the case for the likes of Kleenex, Kodak, and Xerox, for whom such positioning was once a distinct advantage.

In the current market space, however, a first-mover position no longer guarantees success. An example of this is Prodigy, an internet service which, despite being first to market, was soon overtaken by the likes of America Online because Prodigy's platform was developed without much thought for their customers' needs (Hargadon & Douglas, 2001). While both services offered graphical user interfaces (i.e., GUI) to their subscribers long before web browsers were common, AOL sought to be more interactive and intuitive while Prodigy was more content- and text-intensive. Aside from a core of "techies," most users preferred the simpler interface.

Of course AOL has since had its own issues. After peaking at 26.7 million subscribers in 2002, by the end of 2011 AOL was down to only 3.5 million users, while overall internet usage during that time shot up (Lilly, 2011). Much of the slide can be attributed to not having the right strategy to manage the evolution of broadband internet and the decline of dial-up.

This dilemma does not, however, just impact internet companies. As previously mentioned, the Kodak name and brand is almost ubiquitously associated with film photography. Just about everyone knows that the phrase "Kodak moment" describes a photo-worthy event. Unfortunately, the category disruption caused by digital photography has made it difficult for Kodak to find its place in the new market. While it has made a valiant effort to keep up, the company was still forced to file Chapter 11 bankruptcy in January 2012 (McCarty & Jinks, 2012). Whether Kodak will be able to exit bankruptcy is largely dependent on whether the company can develop the right strategy to compete in a market that is drastically different from what it was just a few years before.

Clearly, having a strategy that properly positions an organization to perform is very important. However, while the last few pages have provided excellent examples of why a strategy is important, these examples do not explicitly define strategy. There is no shortage of competing definitions, but all of these variations could be amalgamated into a single definition that is something like *a strategy is a plan that creates sustainable competitive advantage and allows an organization to perform over time, even in the face of a changing environment.* This is the definition that we will use for this discussion.

Strategy is a lot like singing in that many people think they can do it, only a few people can do it well, and most of those who cannot do it well are unaware of how bad they are. It is almost impossible to find a website for even the smallest consulting firm that does not offer some kind of strategic planning services. It takes very little effort, however, to realize that many of these firms have extremely liberal definitions of strategy. The degree to which they deviate from established practice can range from simple issues of nomenclature to borderline negligence. One of the best way to avoid getting caught up in traps like this is to have a full understanding of what strategy is and is not, and of how it can be applied.

Before beginning that discussion, however, two level sets are required. The first level set is that, while there are numerous approaches to strategy formulation, this discussion will draw from three broad categories:

- Competitive environment-focused approaches

- Capabilities-focused approaches

- Customer-focused approaches

While just about every strategic planning model claims to be unique, the truth is that the majority of strategy formulation processes can fit into one of these three categories. More importantly, these approaches represent the three main kinds of data that organizations must consider in their strategic planning efforts. Interestingly, most of the existing approaches use only one of these three domains as the primary unit of analysis. This can lead to an incomplete understanding of the organization and its ecosystem, which in turn can lead to a misaligned strategy. The model discussed later in this book attempts to address that shortcoming.

The second level set is that the remainder of this discussion will be guided by two assumptions:

- Strategy is about creating sustainable advantage

- Strategy formulation efforts should be deliberative

The support for the first assumption has already been discussed and ties back to the definition of strategy. The reason for the second assumption is that there is significant research, including the study this book is based on, suggesting that the goals and objectives of deliberatively formulated strategies tend to be realized more often than those of strategies that just happen to evolve (Brown, 2007; Hrebinaik & Joyce, 2001; Mintzberg, 1987).

While there are various opinions as to why this is the case, the most likely drivers are Case Western University professors Cooperrider and Sekerka's theories that organizations tend to evolve in the direction toward which they focus their attention and energies (2003). While this discussion won't get into the hows and whys of that, it is sufficient to say that all the top-performing organizations that participated in this study indicated that their strategy efforts were deliberative. Truth be told, there aren't too many examples of organizations that have succeeded without being focused and deliberative. There are, however, quite a few examples of organizations that have failed and later admitted that they were largely unfocused.

Now that the bases of what strategy is and how it applies to organizations have been covered, it is time to start talking about how to use these concepts to make organizations better. That is where chapter 3 begins.

3: The Competitive Environment: Looking Outward

Michael Porter is the Bishop William Lawrence University Professor at Harvard Business School, and one of the most popular writers on the topic of the competitive environment as it relates to business strategy. His book *Competitive Strategy* is often cited, and there aren't too many MBAs who don't bring up his Five Forces model at some point when they are starting down the path of strategic planning.

Unfortunately, however, Porter has become so ubiquitous in the strategy discussion that there are some people who try to leverage his theories based on second- or third hand knowledge. In other words, they have heard someone else talk about them but may not have actually read anything that Porter has written. As a result, there is a surprisingly large number of people who are misinformed about what Porter has (or more importantly has not) said.

In Porter's own words, "The essence of formulating a competitive strategy is relating a company to its environment" (1980). He later clarified this view when he said that organizations need to base their strategies on what they can do that is unique compared to their competitors (1996). The focus here is how organizations assess their external environment and use those insights to distinguish themselves in the marketplace. In other words, how do they position themselves relative to their competitors and other factors in their ecosystem?

This externally focused approach has become to go-to concept for many executives. As a Senior Vice President once told me, "We look out at what is going on in the market and figure out how to be better than the other guy. Plain and simple." While the reality is not always quite so simple, the point is valid.

Though Porter is by far the most well-known advocate of this outward-looking approach, he is not the only one. For example, Bruce Greenwald of Columbia Business School and Judd Kahn of Hummingbird Management advocate a combative metaphor that focuses almost exclusively on competing organizations, and claim that the way to ensure success is to figure out how to outmaneuver and defeat the competition (2005).

Kim and Mauborgne of INSEAD also focus on competing organizations, but propose that a combative approach is unproductive and recommend understanding where these competitors are, then going where they are not (2005). Kim and Mauborgne refer to this as a *blue ocean* strategy and basically recommend an avoidance approach, with which organizations succeed by steering clear of direct confrontation.

While both of these approaches purport to offer newer perspectives than Porter's original work, they are in reality simple derivations and limited extensions of Porter's externally focused model rather than unique ways of understanding how strategies are developed and implemented. In addition, they do not consider several other key influencers that the

Five Forces model takes into account. As such, the remainder of this discussion will focus on the more robust progenitor of these externally focused approaches, i.e., Porter and his Five Forces framework.

Porter's Five Forces model is intended to define the state of competition in a given industry. In this model, competition is not limited to other companies that may be battling the organization for resources and share, but includes any entity in the environment that may potentially impact the organization's ability to succeed. For example, the bargaining power of customers and suppliers is considered to be competitive forces as they are external forces that impact the organization's ability to succeed. As such, the focus here is on any external force that impacts the organization, not just direct competitors in the same market space. Figure 1 illustrates this model.

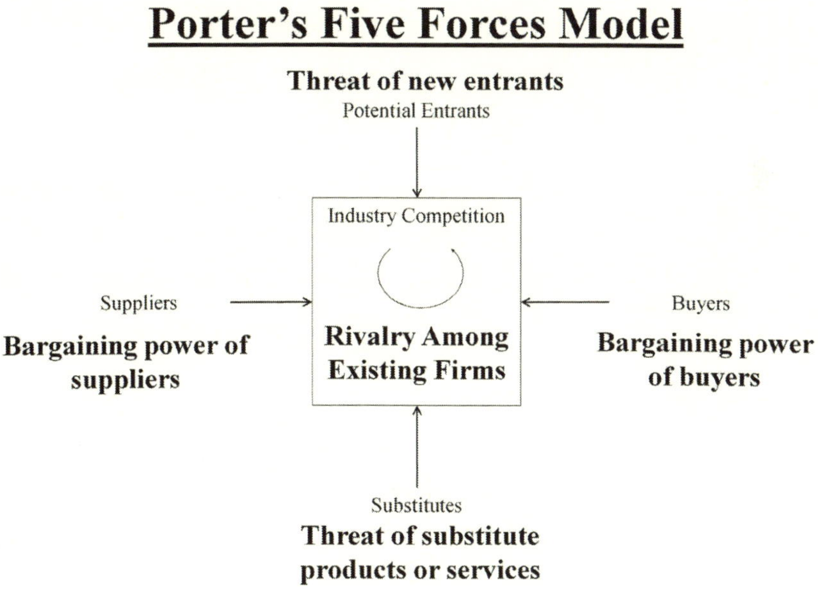

Porter's Five Forces Model

Threat of new entrants
Potential Entrants

Industry Competition

Suppliers → **Rivalry Among Existing Firms** ← Buyers

Bargaining power of suppliers

Bargaining power of buyers

Substitutes
Threat of substitute products or services

Figure 1. Porter's Five Forces Model

- Threat of New Entrants: The threat of potential new entrants into a market is dependent on both the barriers to entry and the potential reaction from the existing competitors in that market space. If the barriers to entry are high, and/or the existing competitors are likely to react adversarially, the likelihood of a new entrant in that market is low. Issues such as high capital requirements for market entry, high switching costs for customers, and governmental regulations can impact the barriers to entry

- Rivalries Among Existing Firms: Rivalries among existing firms develop when one or more firms in a space feel pressure from the other firms in that space or see an opportunity to improve their own position. Rivalries can take the form of tactics such as price competition, advertising battles, new product introductions, and increased customer services and warranties. Ironically, the firm that initiates these actions may not be the one that eventually benefits, and it is possible that the entire industry could suffer if these actions are taken too far

- Threat of Substitute Products or Services: If customers do not buy an organization's products and services, it will not be able to compete against its rivals. In extreme circumstances, substitutions from outside the established supply chains limit the entire industry's potential performance

- Bargaining Power of Buyers: The more bargaining power buyers have, the more challenging it will be for an organization to be successful versus its competitors. The more options buyers have at their disposal, the more bargaining power they have. Standardized products, low switching costs, capacity for backward integration, and more informed buyers all increase this power base

- Bargaining Power of Suppliers: Suppliers can impact the performance of participants in a particular industry when they adjust the price or quality of the inputs to an organization's production process. These conditions are more likely to occur when there are fewer suppliers and competition for their resources becomes more scarce among the organizations in that industry

The idea behind the Five Forces model is that the collective strength of these five external forces determines how much potential opportunity there is in the market. Once opportunity is identified, that is where the organization should focus its strategy. For example, an industry that has few existing competitors, few potential new entrants, and low bargaining power among buyers would be considered to have a large amount of opportunity. It would make sense to focus the organization's strategy and efforts on such an industry.

On the other hand, an industry that already has an abundance of competitors, thereby resulting in commoditization of the product or service and an increase in the bargaining power of purchasers, would be seen as having less opportunity. It would be unwise for an organization to develop a strategy that focuses on such an industry. In both cases, however, the issue is how does the organization position itself in its competitive environment?

According to Porter, surface-level understanding of these forces is often readily apparent to anyone who is competing, or thinking about competing, in a given space (1980). The problem, however, is that a surface-level understanding isn't sufficient to be able to understand how to properly position the organization for success. To develop sustainable competitive advantage, an organization must dive below the surface to fully comprehend each of these forces and how they are related to the organization. This next level of analysis is one that organizations often skip, resulting in incomplete or inaccurate conclusions.

Regardless of the depth of analysis performed or the amount of opportunity identified, the information gleaned from these analyses is then used to make decisions about how the organization wants to try to position itself in its environment. According to Porter, there are three primary positions that an organization can choose from (2001):

- Variety-based positioning: Deciding to focus on a subset of an industry's products or services. Makes the most sense when an organization can best produce particular products or services using a distinctive set of activities

- Needs-based positioning: Deciding to serve most or all of the needs of a particular group of customers. This kind of positioning is only truly effective if what the organization is providing is a product or service that meets customers' needs better than competitors' offerings

- Access-based positioning: Deciding to provide products or services to customers in markets that may not have access to other options. The challenge with this approach is that it is often difficult to provide these services cost-effectively, hence the reason for lack of competitors. Making this kind of positioning work is not impossible, but may require some creativity

Typically an organization will only select one of these positions. By adopting a particular position, an organization is trying to carve out a niche that distinguishes itself from its rivals. The challenge, according to Porter, is that finding a unique position is not in and of itself a way to create sustainable competitive advantage.

If an organization takes some new position and is successful at it, competitors will take notice. They will then try to understand what the first organization did to gain that advantage and may attempt to copy it. If the position is easy to duplicate, they likely will. This scenario will quickly erode the original organization's advantage. There a numerous examples where small organizations make some breakthrough that is then copied and exploited by larger firms with more resources. Porter points to technology-based industries as an avenue where this has happened consistently, and where a well thought out strategy for how to handle these kinds of situations is critical for ongoing success (2001). The recent efforts of organizations like Google and Yahoo to create social media engines to compete with Facebook further illustrates this point.

When trying to create a competitive advantage, organizations often need to make what Porter refers to as trade-offs, which will allow them to exploit one position even when it is at the expense of another position (1996). Trade-offs are those hard decisions that purposefully limit what the organization offers. They are also the decisions that the organization hopes will make it hard for competitors to duplicate an organization's success.

Porter cites organizations such as Southwest Airlines, Neutrogena Corporation (a skincare company), and Ikea as entities that have made the trade-offs to focus on their particular niches and have been very successful. They did so by choosing to differentiate themselves by focusing on a particular area, even though it meant giving up potentially broader markets. In the case of Southwest Airlines, they gave up focusing on business travelers, who are typically willing to pay higher fares. In doing so, they chose to focus on the value traveler, creating a niche in the airline market that was largely untapped up to that time.

This goes back to the earlier discussion of Kim and Mauborgne's *blue ocean* strategy (2005). The organization chooses to diverge from the competition and focus on a different segment, all but creating a new market. While this approach has been effective for some organizations, it is not uncommon for the benefits to be temporary. Other organizations may attempt to move into these new markets once they recognize that those markets can be lucrative.

The Wall Street Journal reported in 2006 how Whole Foods was facing this exact challenge. Their market share in the high-end grocery business, which they basically created, was eroding as a result of this very paradigm (McDonald & Admay, 2006). While Whole Foods is obviously still around, it is not hard to see that they are no longer the only option, and as such have lost their *blue ocean* type advantage. They must look for other ways to remain competitive.

Despite these and other problems, the externally focused approach to strategy remains popular. By Porter's own accounts, this model focuses on making decisions based primarily on competitors and the environment (1996; 1998; 2001). While taking these factors into account is important, doing so creates a situation where organizations are making decisions in reaction to elements that they cannot directly control. Moreover, markets and competition can change extremely quickly compared to the time it takes to develop and implement a strategy. This paradox has some managers thinking that the externally focused approach is too slow and too reactive to meet their needs.

Taking such an approach also requires organizations to base critical decisions almost entirely on what their *enemies* are doing. Returning to the previously mentioned wisdom of Sun Tzu, there is evidence that making movements based solely upon the actions of opponents can be unwise (Griffith, 1963). While it is important to consider this information, an alternative approach might be to start off reviewing the organization's strengths, and then determine how to exploit those advantages in terms of what the competition is doing. This is what some leaders refer to as the core capabilities approach, which is the focus of the next chapter.

4: Leveraging Internal Capabilities

While focusing on the competitive environment is by far the most popular approach, there is growing recognition that it may not be the best option for developing strategic advantage. As early as 1992, the *Harvard Business Review* was publishing articles that identified *capabilities* as the differentiator that enabled companies like Walmart and Honda to outperform their rivals (Stalk & Shulman, 1992). While not discounting consideration of the external environment, the capabilities-based approach sees internal focus as the primary unit of analysis and the best place to direct the strategy discussion.

One of the main tenets of this view is that the success of an organization is dependent on transforming its key processes into strategic capabilities that provide superior value to the marketplace. This focus on the key areas of concern is very similar to the idea of the critical few versus the trivial many concept that can be found in process improvement methodologies such as statistical process control and six sigma (Carey & Lloyd, 2001). There is also growing recognition that there is more to capabilities than just hard assets like equipment and distribution channels. Capabilities can be intangible assets such as branding, goodwill, and methodologies for managing customers.

Two of the best recognized proponents of this approach are Gary Hamel and C.K. Prahalad. Gary Hamel is currently the director of the Woodside Institute and a visiting professor of strategic management at London Business School. Until his passing in 2010, C.K. Prahalad was a Distinguished University Professor of Corporate Strategy at the University of Michigan. Interestingly, these two men often published as a team. They agree with Porter that the goal of strategy is to create sustainable competitive advantage. Where they disagree with Porter, however, is where they think the conversation should begin. They are of the opinion that organizations should think about competitive advantage in terms of what they refer to as *core competencies*. Core competencies, according to Hamel and Prahalad, are a bundle of skills and technologies that enable the organization to provide a particular benefit to its customers (1994). In other words, those differentiating capabilities that make the organization who and what it is.

The commitment an organization makes to building core competencies is a commitment to create or further perfect its ability to deliver benefits to customers. It isn't necessarily a commitment to some specific product or market opportunity; it is a decision to focus on a certain way of delivering what customers want. This focus includes not just *what* the organization does, but also *how* it undertakes the activities that drive those outcomes.

Properly developed core competencies can stay constant and consistently add value across product and service categories. Figure 2 illustrates this concept.

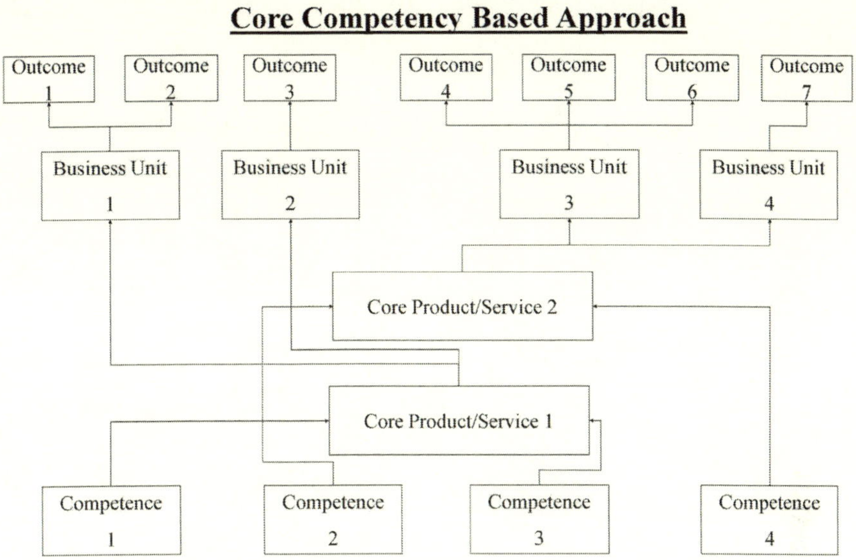

Core Competency Based Approach

```
[Outcome 1] [Outcome 2] [Outcome 3]    [Outcome 4] [Outcome 5] [Outcome 6] [Outcome 7]
      |           |           |              |           |           |           |
  [Business Unit 1]    [Business Unit 2]   [Business Unit 3]      [Business Unit 4]
                              |
                     [Core Product/Service 2]
                              |
                     [Core Product/Service 1]
                              
  [Competence 1]   [Competence 2]   [Competence 3]        [Competence 4]
```

Figure 2. Illustration of Hamel and Prahalad's Core Competency-Based Approach

To understand this model, it is important to fully understand what capabilities are. It is also important to understand what competencies are, as well as how the two differ.

While capabilities have been described in a number of ways, this discussion will define capabilities as "the collective skills, abilities, and expertise of an organization" (Ulrich & Smallwood, 2004). Even with a clean definition like this, however, it is not uncommon for there to be some confusion between capabilities and competencies. This confusion is problematic for discussions like this because it can create misunderstanding of what people are talking about.

Reducing these misunderstandings requires explicit criteria for what makes core competencies distinctly unique. To clarify this differentiation,

Hamel and Prahalad provide three tests that a capability must pass to be considered a *core competency*:

- Does the capability make a disproportionate contribution to the ultimate customer value, and/or does it allow the company to deliver value to customers in an appreciably more efficient way?

- Does the particular capability provide a potential basis for entry into some new market?

- Is this capability difficult for competitors to imitate?

So how is the determination made that a capability is disproportionately contributing to the ultimate customer or delivering value to customers in an appreciably more efficient way? This is pretty much a judgment call based on the organization's goals, but Hamel and Prahalad use McDonald's to illustrate the point.

They posit that it is McDonald's ability to create a unique customer experience, beyond just the quality of the food, that lets the organization deliver value to the customer in a unique way (1992). While there are other restaurant chains that have comparable or better menus, it is the experience created by things like speed of service, convenience, the Ronald McDonald character, and Happy Meals that make the difference and drive customers to the Golden Arches over other alternatives. If you don't believe this, just ask the parent of a young child how often they go to McDonald's and why. Unless they are someone who just happens to be completely opposed to fast food, there is a pretty good chance they will say they are there more often than they would like to be, and it isn't for the taste of the food. As such, this capability passes the first test of being a core competency.

The next question of whether is qualifies as a core competency is the degree to which that capability provides a basis for entry into a new market. While Hamel and Prahalad provide several examples of this, the one that best exemplifies this criterion could be Walmart (1994). Walmart has the capacity to leverage information technology so that they can manage their supply chain with so much efficiency that they can offer their products at much lower prices than their competitors. They have been able to use this capability to expand into other markets and replicate their success at an exponential rate. By leveraging this ever-growing network, Walmart has created a core competency that is difficult for competitors to imitate. Walmart is thereby able to maintain their strategic advantage in the market. Interestingly, their ability to manage this considerable and distributed supply chain has allowed them to become so large that it is very difficult for any competitor to catch up. A big part of staying successful is making sure your competitors either do not learn from your success, or cannot imitate it even if they do.

This leads to the third test: is the capability difficult for competitors to imitate? This is one place where Hamel and Prahalad are in complete agreement with Porter's view that organizations can only outperform rivals if they can establish a differentiation point that can be preserved over time.

One of the best examples of this dynamic is the pharmaceuticals industry, where competitive advantage is created based on superior products (i.e., new and better drugs). That advantage can only be maintained so long as a particular product's patent protection is in place. Since figuring out the chemical compound of a drug is a relatively simple matter, patent protection is the only thing that prevents competitors from copying the formulation and releasing their own drug for the same ailment.

As soon as the patent protection expires, competitors produce generic versions of the original drug. The generic versions then flood the market and commoditization begins. With commoditization, the differences between generics and the name brand become much less relevant, and consumers begin making decisions based on price. Prices for the generic versions are typically much less than the branded version because generic manufacturers did not incur the heavy development costs of the name-brand manufacturer. At this point the competitive advantage of the name-brand product quickly erodes. Obviously, capabilities that are difficult to imitate are critically important.

Developing capabilities that are difficult to imitate can be costly and time-consuming. Organizations must seriously evaluate the strategic value of a particular capability before deciding to make the investment required to turn it into a core competency. While the book value of assets developed from these investments may not deteriorate with use and age like physical assets, and in some cases can grow over time, they do require continuous review and maintenance to persist in adding value. Organization must consciously devote not only money but also time to growing them.

British Airways is an example of an organization that chose to do this when it differentiated itself by offering superior service, even though the costs of developing the core competencies associated with that capability ended up being significant, both in terms of time and money (Iacobucci, 1996; Prokesch, 1995; Weiser, 1995). It did this in a number of ways, including new aircraft and increased services to its passengers. By making this commitment, however, British Airways has developed a strategic advantage that it is able to maintain, even when the unique aspects of the airline market evolve and change. This ability to maintain advantage, even in the face of changing market spaces, is one of the keys to developing a sustainable competitive advantage.

Complicating this issue is the fact that it is becoming more difficult for organizations to differentiate themselves from their competitors based just on product features and benefits. The environment, which is what positioning is concerned with, may change practically overnight. This was the case with the introduction of the Internet, or the implosion of the resulting technology bubble in the late nineties and early 2000s.

Maintaining the uniqueness of features and benefits, which core competencies contribute to, is also becoming more difficult. The *cycle time* during which product or service benefits can remain unique, continues to become shorter, and the barriers for entry of new competitors in many markets are becoming lower.

This begs the question: what are best-in-class organizations doing to differentiate themselves in the marketplace? Evidence is mounting that it is the intangible assets, such as customer relationships, that are making the difference in the performance of organizations. The truly successful organizations are the ones that focus attention on developing and managing those assets. That is the focus of the next chapter.

5: It's About the Customer...

Despite how preposterous it sounds, viewing customer management as a critical input is a relatively new direction for business strategies. While many organizations have long offered platitudes about focusing on their customers, saying that and actually driving businesses decisions based on that are often two very different things. Surely just about everyone reading this book has had experiences, both as a customer and as an employee, in which an organization has put their own needs far ahead of their customers'. Need an example? Go to any airport and find someone who just got bumped from an oversold flight.

The simple fact is that customers are becoming more demanding, and organizations must be more mindful of those demands if they want to maintain market leadership. This doesn't mean that organizations have to acquiesce to every demand that every customer makes. Doing so would drive up the cost of delivery to unmanageable levels. What it does mean, however, is that organizations must actively manage the customer experience and be more mindful of how customers perceive that experience.

Complicating this issue are the growth of the information economy and the increasing number of well-informed (or, in some cases, misinformed) consumers. Social media outlets such as Facebook and Twitter have created portals for customers to quickly share any experiences with large numbers of connections. As has always been the case, they are much more likely to share bad experiences than good ones. It is therefore becoming more important for organizations to be active rather than passive in how they manage their relationships with their customers.

Even before the rise of social media, markets had evolved to the point where it had become difficult for a company to maintain a leadership position. For example, between 1972 and 2002, the likelihood that companies in leadership positions in their particular markets would lose those positions more than doubled (Viguerie & Thompson, 2005). If the anecdotal data in the business press is any indication, those challenges have only increased in recent years.

There are, however, several examples of organizations that have been able to not only survive their evolving markets, but also thrive by focusing on their customers. Harley-Davidson, Southwest Airlines, the Body Shop, and Patagonia have all become successful by focusing not just on *what* they provide to their customers (i.e., the tangibles), but also *how* they provide those services and products (i.e., the intangibles).

While product quality cannot be ignored, lack of defects alone is not a differentiator that drives success. Otherwise, Harley-Davidson would be no different from Honda or Suzuki; Southwest would be no different from US Airways or United; the Body Shop would be losing sales to Kmart's generic products; and Patagonia would be no different from the dozens of other companies that make heavy coats.

There are numerous examples of organizations that are developing strategies to manage intangible assets effectively. Robert Kaplan of

Harvard Business School and David Norton of the Balanced Scorecard Collective provide an excellent illustration of how the North American Marketing and Refining (NAM&R) arm of ExxonMobile improved operating cash flow by more than $1 billion a year, in large part by focusing on their customers' needs and finding ways to meet those needs (2001). While at first glance the details of this example may suggest that NAM&R's approach was more aligned with the capabilities-based line of thinking advocated by Hamel and Prahalad, the difference here is where the company chose to focus. It looked first at who its customers were, and then tried to figure out how to enhance or build competencies to support those customers.

The casino gaming division of Harrah's Entertainment (now part of Caesar's Entertainment) used a variety of customer segmentation and analytic techniques to identify who their most valuable customers were and then adjusted the organization's strategy to focus on those customers' needs (Gulati & Oldroyd, 2005; Sutton & Klein, 2003). What they found was that most of their revenue came not from the big spenders that the gaming industry had historically focused on, but from middle-income and retiree gamers who were largely ignored by the competition. Harrah's shifted their service and marketing strategies to concentrate on this underserved yet high-revenue segment of the market. By changing their focus to better serve this customer segment, Harrah's was able to create substantial growth, even in a weak economy (Loveman, 2003; Sutton & Klein, 2003).

NAM&R and Harrah's engaged in different strategies to improve their performance by understanding their customers' unique needs and adjusting accordingly. Both organizations saw great success from their efforts, and continue to grow because of it. What do these approaches have in common? The answer is that they both began by focusing on the customers, and then explored how to meet those customers' needs.

An excellent customer service strategy can drive high satisfaction, resulting in more new customers, more transactions from existing customers, fewer lost customers, and more insulation from the competition. It is all but conventional wisdom that it is easier and less expensive to retain and grow existing customers than it is to acquire new customers. Effectively and consistently meeting customer needs can drive customer loyalty, which can result not only in increased sales, but also in customers who enthusiastically promote those products and services they are loyal to. When a customer promotes an organization's products, it costs the organization significantly less money to generate sales. All of these facts make providing high quality service an imperative to many organizations.

It should be noted, however, that not everyone is convinced that gaining customer loyalty is the end all and be all of business goals. Reinartz and Kumar's 2002 article in the *Harvard Business Review* points out that there are times when more loyal customers may actually be more expensive to serve. The issue seems to be that more loyal customers tend to become more educated about the products and services they are purchasing. As a result, they might be able to "game the system" so as to get more value from a company at less cost to themselves. Frequent flyers, for example, may take great pride in all but abusing their program status for perks and benefits, even if it ends up costing the airline money.

While this is a valid concern, Reinartz and Kumar themselves admit that this challenge can be addressed by not providing high quality services to just anyone, but by focusing on providing high quality services to the right customers. This is similar to the Harrah's example, in which the organization decided not to worry about the "whales" who expected to be coddled by the casinos at great expense, could in some cases abuse the system, and could significantly hurt the casino if they started winning. Instead, Harrah's focused on middle-income customers and retirees who were more appreciative and more economical to serve (Loveman, 2003; Sutton & Klein, 2003). Approaches like this can be implemented by using the right customer segmentation model to understand how to slice and dice an organization's market.

Customer segmentation is about identifying distinct customer groups that have homogenous needs. The goal is to develop strategies around the needs of the most important groups, so that resources can be effectively applied to serving the right customers and thereby generate the maximum benefit for the company. Both the ExxonMobile NAM&R and Harrah's Entertainment examples illustrate organizations using a segmentation approach to better understand what different groups of customers desired and developing strategies to serve them more effectively (Kaplan & Norton, 2001; Loveman, 2003; Sutton & Klein, 2003).

While this approach is more common in business-to-consumer organizations, many business-to-business organizations also understand the need to develop and define manageable segments. Medical equipment supplier Hill-Rom was able to recover lost market share by segmenting their customers and developing effective strategies to manage those segments (Waaser, Dahneke, Pekkarinen, & Weissel, 2004). Some studies have shown that the impact of properly executed, segmentation based strategies on profitability can be anywhere from a 20–85% increase (Payne & Frow, 1999).

Of course, once a segmentation scheme is developed, the appropriate strategy for serving those segments must be formulated. While a high-level scan of the business literature might lead one to think that this issue has been all figured out, a deeper dive reveals that most of the advice is either anecdotal or an advertisement for some consulting firm's particular offerings. There is the even greater problem that the service approaches that do exist seem to focus on the customer as though that customer exists in a vacuum, apart from the rest of the organization's ecosystem. There is no consideration of how to apply segmentation data in light of what the competition is doing or what capabilities the organization might have.

Taking a holistic view that considers the entire ecosystem can be accomplished by applying the concept of systems thinking. This application is the focus of the next chapter.

6: Systems Thinking

Systems thinking is not quite as well known and overused as strategy, but it is close. A Google search on *systems thinking* returns around 284 million results. Narrowing the search to *systems theory* only cuts the results down to 189 million. Clearly there is a lot of thought about this concept, but what is it that all these people talking about?

At its most basic level, *systems thinking* is a process for looking at some entity—in this case, an organization. The main differentiator of systems thinking is that it takes a holistic view of the entity being considered and tries to understand the entity as a coherent unit within its ecosystem, rather than just breaking the entity down into its component parts without considering the interrelatedness of those parts. Systems thinking is one of the foundations of organizational development and change management, and, much like strategic planning, it has multiple viewpoints.

One side views organizations as open systems that are in active exchange with their environment (French & Bell, 1999). Another side focuses on understanding the full patterns of behavior of the various parts of the organization as an interactive whole (Senge, 2006). This is the view found in Peter Senge's well-known *The Fifth Discipline*. Both systems thinking approaches are alternatives to the more common reductionist methodologies that break concepts into smaller and smaller components for the sake of analysis and understanding, but sometimes fail to link those components back together in a way that creates a complete picture of the organization and the environment in which it operates. It is this failure to relink the parts and understand the whole that drives many of the confusion points and miscalculations found in business today.

Systems thinking has been used to tackle a wide variety of subjects in fields such as computing, engineering, epidemiology, information science, health, manufacturing, management, and the environment. Despite this variety of applications, there has not been much effort to apply systems thinking to strategic planning. While some texts, such as *The Dance of Change* (Senge et. al., 1999), have touched on the idea of how systems thinking can be applied to strategy, most of these discussions have been anecdotal at best and do not provide much insight as to how systems thinking can be applied to organizations looking to improve their strategic planning activities. This is surprising, given that systems thinking has been shown to be valuable in helping address complex issues. As seen in the previous chapters, effective strategic planning requires taking multiple, complex, and sometimes conflicting dynamics into account.

The goal of systems thinking is to understand interrelationships and patterns, rather than just snapshots and static single points of data. This is in contrast to many strategic planning efforts that often end up focusing on finite facts and figures, usually driven by the Chief Financial Officer. An approach to strategic planning that incorporates a systems thinking approach could respond to the contention that strategy planning models often focus too much on those single perspectives.

Every organization is different. With the exception of a few key metrics (usually financial), so are the data points that get incorporated into the strategic planning process. While there may be some common metrics across a particular industry (e.g., number of prescriptions written in the pharmaceutical space) the exact data used to develop a strategic plan may vary wildly, even among close competitors. And even when the meaning of the data is similar, the terminology used to describe those data can vary widely from organization to organization.

Despite this disparity, there are a few things that can be realistically assumed to be common across all organizations. First, all organizations must consider the external (i.e., competitive) environment when formulating and executing their strategies. The reason for this is there are numerous external factors that influence whether a customer does or does not purchase from a particular organization. If those factors are not reacted to properly, the organization can quickly lose its position of advantage in the market.

The second assumption is that organizations must take a good, hard look at their core competencies to understand how they will execute on their objectives to meet the needs of their customers. In addition, it is important to be able to differentiate between the core competencies that add value versus the multiple capabilities that are just part of the ongoing business process. Making those distinctions is a vital driver in the hard decisions about where and how to invest.

The third assumption is that organizations must take their customers into account. After all, the customer base is why the organization exists. A frequent question is what if an organization is not-for-profit or a government entity? Simply replace the word *customer* with *stakeholders*, *constituents*, or whatever word is most applicable to the population whose needs the organization exists to meet. What group would be in need if the organization had never been created?

Taking these three assumptions into account, the research project that drove this effort involved applying a systems thinking view to the various case studies and examples in the business and academic literature to develop a strategy model that would explain what was common across successful organizations. Developing that model involved many hours in front of a whiteboard, at least two packages of dry erase markers, and more iterations than anyone would care to count. The end result was a model that reflects the trends in the literature. That model is shown in Figure 3.

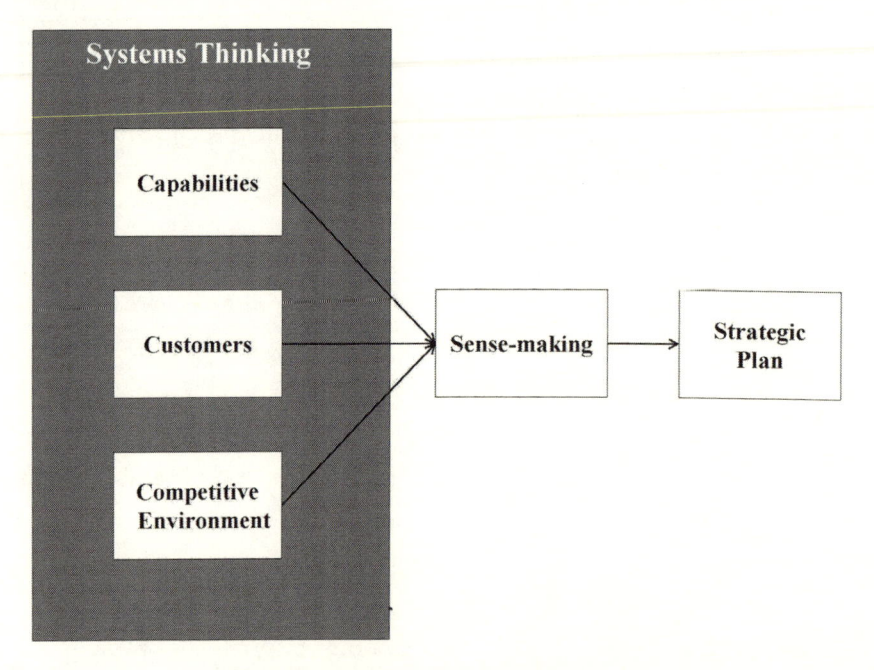

Figure 3. Systems Thinking Strategy

There are several important points to be made about the Systems Thinking Strategy (STS) model that is presented in Figure 3. First, it reflects a finalized and refined version of the model that resulted from the study, not the model that was tested during that research project. The dissertation took more than 2,300 words and several graphics to describe the process of developing the model that was tested. Here that description was trimmed to just a few paragraphs.

Second, the model that was tested was referred to in the research study, and in the research notes of this book, as the Multi-Dimensional Strategy Model. The models are the same, but the name was changed after the completion of the original study to reflect the criticality of systems thinking in the process. It is also important to note the order of the three categories of data and the box that reads "Sense-Making" between those data categories and the "Strategic Plan" box.

The categories of data are specifically ordered: *Capabilities* at the top, *Customers* in the middle, and *Competitive Environment* at the bottom. The reason for this is that the organizations that participated in this study reported taking *Capabilities* into account in their strategic planning efforts the most often. *Customers* were taken into account second most often, and the *Competitive Environment* was third. This does not, however, mean that any of these categories of data should be dismissed, as the research does show that successful organizations consider all three perspectives. What it does mean, however, is that the priority of the consideration is important and may challenge some of the predominant thinking.

While the competition focused approaches are by far the most popular, the findings of this study suggest that it is not necessarily the most productive or most important. Sociologists could provide some fascinating insights as to why many business articles and books are so focused on the competitive aspects and what it means for the state of the current business climate and society in general, but that is outside of the scope of this discussion. The point here is that all the dynamics need to be considered. Collectively, they provide a way to understand and apply the data points, which is often lacking.

Sense-making was not covered in chapters 2 through 5, and readers may be wondering where that box came from. After many hours staring at the aforementioned whiteboard and thumbing through the various research articles to try to understand not only the what, but also the how and why of this process, it became apparent that there was a major gap in many of the models. While most models focused on how organizations get from here to there, few if any talked about how organizations decide where "there" really should be. The sense-making box was added to the research model to account for this glaring gap, and an effort to elicit information about those processes was added to the data collection plan.

While the likes of Porter and Hamel and Prahalad have hinted at this issue by offering different perspectives on the kinds of data that should be incorporated into decisions, most organizations still seem to be making strategic decisions based on what is sometimes referred to as *intuitive synthesis* (Khatri, 1994). Other terms for this approach that get tossed around conference rooms are "trusting your gut," or the more sophisticated sounding "experiential judgment." Regardless of what it is called, this approach seems to be the most popular methodology not just in strategic planning, but in many business decisions. While it has stood the test of time due to its simplicity and wide range of applications, it is not well understood and not very reliable. As such, a better approach is required. The approach described here draws heavily from behavioral scientists' and psychologists' understanding of cognitive processes.

Sense-making is an attempt by individuals to explain sets of clues from their environments, whether internal or external, and use that data to make decisions. This process is of critical importance in organizations, as there is evidence of a link between the quality of these sense-making activities and business outcomes (Maitlis, 2005; Thomas, Clark, & Giola, 1993). There does not, however, appear to be a strategy model that explicitly takes this process into account. This is why sense-making was added.

Sense-making is a key component of the systems thinking strategy model—one of the things that makes it unique when compared to other alternatives. Chapter 10 will provide much more insight into the details of these activities.

As already discussed, the research that this book is based upon was written in full academic voice and provided lots of detail about how the model that became the STS was developed, tested, and refined. It included lots of facts, figures, and data. In short, it showed all the math. There are abbreviated research notes at the end of this text for those who are interested. For immediate purposes, however, a few points of information about the study are relevant.

The project involved gathering and analyzing feedback from 66 top-performing organizations. These organizations were all publicly traded and had to meet at least one of two criteria for high performance: either they were one of the top 200 organizations in terms of stock price performance for the five years prior to the start of the study, or they were listed in the Fortune 500 for the previous year.

Analysis of the feedback from these 66 organization included both quantitative and qualitative approaches. The quantitative approaches included a review of descriptive statistics of the data to determine if patterns of behavior existed and the directions of those, as well as chi-squared (χ^2) tests to determine if those patterns were statistically significant. In each case, the findings were very statistically significant.

The qualitative approaches looked into the details of what was going into those organizations' strategic efforts and sought to gain a deeper perspective on how they were using their data and how they made sense of them.

Certain commonalities presented themselves which helped explain not just the what, but the how and why of these organizations' strategy efforts. These details are important for any organization that would want to understand how to apply these concepts, and are illustrated in Figure 4.

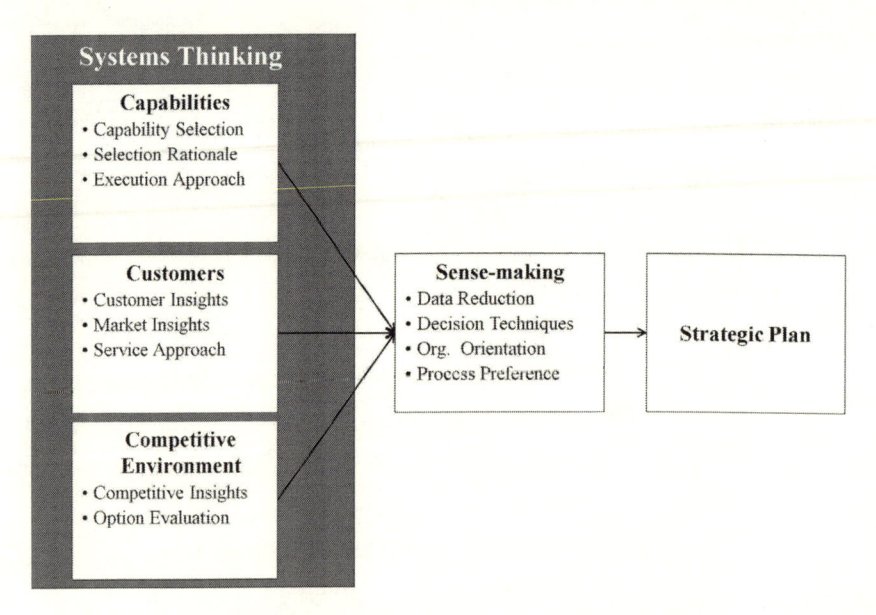

Figure 4. Detailed Systems Thinking Strategy

Obviously there is much more to developing an enhanced strategy model than just saying that it will consider multiple dynamics. Each part of the puzzle has its own issues to consider and needs to be taken into account in the appropriate way. The chapters that follow provide a more detailed understanding of how this can be applied.

7: Applying Capabilities in the STS

It has already been established that the ability to develop and leverage capabilities is a key differentiator in an organization's success. Many high-performing organizations (e.g., Walmart) achieve their success by turning specific capabilities into core competencies that enable them to thrive regardless of the competition's actions or other factors in their environment. So while the capabilities and customer focused approaches are not discussed as much as ones that focus on the competitive environment, an understanding of how to make the right decisions about which capabilities to develop into core competencies is a critical task for an organization's success. Moreover, the top-performing organizations that participated in this study reported incorporating capabilities-based decisions into their strategic planning processes more often than they reported focusing on information about the competitive environment or customers.

Integrating capabilities-based information into strategic planning processes can be challenging. Not only is it less popular than other approaches, but deciding which tradeoffs to make can be hard. In addition, developing capabilities can be both costly and time-consuming. As described in chapter 5, British Airways did not turn itself around overnight. It required many years of concerted effort and heavy investment. More recently, Delta Air Lines has begun to transform itself in a similar manner (Stych, 2012). Although they have made great progress, the process is still ongoing. Developing capabilities into core competencies is a long-term strategic bet that can fly in the face of the quarterly reporting cycles that drive many business decisions today.

Organizations must seriously contemplate the strategic value of the capabilities they want to evolve into core competencies before making investment decisions. Such decisions should not be taken lightly. When looking at the feedback provided by participants in this study, it appears that the process for making these decisions is focused on three main activities:

- Capabilities Selection: Deciding what the organization is (and is not) going to do

- Execution Approach: Deciding how the selected capabilities will be leveraged

- Rationale: The business justification for selecting those capabilities and the method of execution over other options

Figure 5 illustrates the interaction of these three activities. Note that the Rationale is supportive of both the Capabilities Selection and Execution Approach, and that Capabilities Selection tends to inform the Execution Approach decisions. It should also be noted that while the interactions among these activities may appear to be primarily linear, they may be more cyclical in nature. Such would be the case when the viability (or lack thereof) of an Execution Approach may require an organization to reevaluate what capabilities it has selected. That viability would also of course inform the Rationale for the decisions.

Systems Thinking Strategy

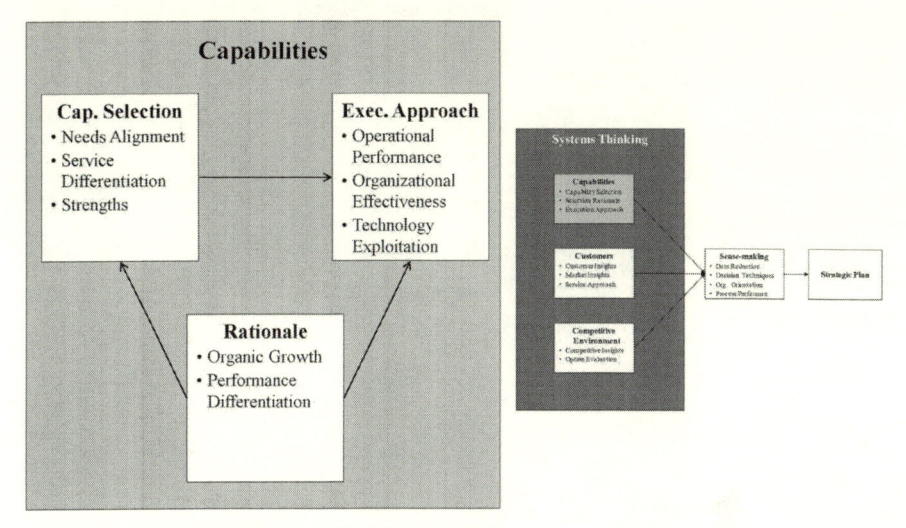

Figure 5. STS Capabilities Component

The first activity that will be discussed in detail is Capabilities Selection. This is when the organization decides what it is (or is not) going to do. This is often one of the most difficult parts of the process. It requires the organization to take a hard look at itself and decide what resources it will invest. This is often referred to as "organizational soul searching." The trick in this effort is to stay focused so that the soul searching does not turn into some kind of navel gazing.

While the particular capabilities that are considered during this process can vary significantly from industry to industry and organization to organization, the approaches used to make these determinations tend to break down into three processes:

- Needs Alignment: Developing a deep understanding of customer and market needs, and then aligning the organization's capabilities to be able to meet those needs in a markedly better way than other provider options

- Service Differentiation: Driving toward capabilities that meet the needs of a specific market segment, even at the risk of losing market share in other segments to whom those capabilities or delivery models may be less appealing

- Strengths: Developing a detailed understanding of the organization's particular strengths and weaknesses, and then looking for places in the market to apply those strengths. Also includes looking for ways to build upon existing strengths

One of the most important parts of this process is the organization being honest with itself about what it is and is not good at. The simple fact is that no organization can be good at everything, even within a single market. For example, Lululemon has made an excellent niche for itself by focusing on the previously underdeveloped market of exercise equipment, athletic wear, and exercise accessories for women (Sacks, 2009). By contrast, HOA Restaurant Group (a.k.a. Hooters) ran into real trouble when they attempted to extend beyond their core competencies of restaurants and adjacent offerings such as calendars, and ventured into the airline business. They lacked any capabilities or experience in that arena, and as a result failed miserably ("Hooters," 2006). An examination of the sample quotes from the participants in this study illustrates how organizations that are performing well are executing the Capabilities Selection process.

Table 1: Capabilities Selection Quotes

Activities	Sample Quotes from Study
Needs Alignment	*Our strategic planning efforts take into consideration our core competencies as well as new value-added services that can be offered to our customers.*
	We have a high focus on our core capabilities and refine our approach to the market to develop and strengthen customer relationships where are capabilities are most needed.
Service Differentiation	*We are not all things to all people, but we are very good at providing services to a narrowly defined niche market. We don't differentiate on product (product is a commodity) but rather on service. Provide a high level of service is our core capability and we structure our organization to be able to provide such a high level of service.*
	We attempt strategically and tactically to develop, over time, as many unique capabilities as possible to gain competitive advantage.
Strengths	*The business strategy is aimed at capitalizing on internal and organizational strengths. Those strengths are then analyzed in the context of the competitive environment and the results of that analysis is used to establish priorities for capital investment, research and development, etc. to strengthen the corporation's core capabilities.*
	Always identifying those things that we do well and those things that we do less well. This process has served us well, helping us to avoid mistakes that we have seen some of our competitors make.

Given that developing these capabilities into core competencies often requires significant investment, the individuals making these decisions must be able to justify them. Despite the popularity of the intuitive synthesis approach described in chapter 6, trusting one's gut is not sufficient when millions of dollars are at risk. The Rationale to support those decisions must be logical and defendable. For the organizations that participated in this study, there seemed to be two primary reasons why particular capabilities were selected:

- Organic Growth: Choosing to drive the development and execution of specific capabilities because they can either increase current share of a particular market, allow the organization to move into a new market now, or allow the organization to grow in a new direction in the future

- Performance Differentiation: Choosing to drive the development and execution of specific capabilities because they allow the organization to deliver products or services that are sufficiently different from competitors

Interestingly, the focus on Organic Growth is contrary to the aggressive growth strategies that many organizations take to meet quarterly performance goals. This approach requires a longer time horizon and what might also be termed organizational bravery to stay the course in the near term. For publicly traded companies, this approach is particularly precarious as it may require short-term losses that may be challenged by shareholders before the investment can produce a return. When an organization is able to ride out these short-term challenges, however, it does appear that these longer-term organic approaches do provide significantly higher stakeholder value.

An examination of the Performance Differentiation approaches show that many successful organizations are looking to make themselves unique in the marketplace rather than going head-to-head with the competition. This is similar to the *blue ocean* approach proposed by Kim and Mauborgne (2005), but differs in terms of the starting point for the analyses. Rather than worrying first about the competition and how to avoid them, the organization begins by looking at their capabilities first, and how those compare to the competition second. Table 2 provides quotes that illustrate these concepts.

Table 2: Rationale Quotes

Rationale	Sample Quotes from Study
Organic Growth	*We have historically focused on leveraging our core technology through new products and applications or distribution of products that are used in the same procedures as our laser-based products. As part of our strategic planning underway, we have begun to consider potentially disruptive technologies that may be a threat to our base business and partner with these potentially disruptive technologies.* *Building a strategy to compete on capabilities that are not currently resident in the company would require time, investment, and reduce probability of success in the short term.*
Performance Differentiation	*We are always focused on driving what makes us DIFFERENT/UNIQUE in our marketplaces. For instance, in one of our divisions it was the combination of security applications and geospatial software that makes us truly unique from our entire competitor set.* *We attempt strategically and tactically to develop, over time, as many unique capabilities as possible to gain competitive advantage.*

Once the capabilities that will be developed into core competencies are selected and the rationale for taking those approaches is documented, the organization has established the *what* of the capabilities portion of its strategy. Next the organization must determine *how* to make those objectives a reality. Deciding on the how influences not only the organization's strategic efforts, but also its day-to-day business activities. Framing of these activities can be described as the Execution Approach. An organization's Execution Approach must consider three focuses:

- Operational Performance: Focusing on efficient and effective execution of core operations, and driving toward outcomes directly resulting from those activities. This includes not only excellence in current operations, but also continuously looking for ways to improve those activities and improve their outcomes

- Organizational Effectiveness: Focusing on leveraging organizational capabilities to drive strong performance. This includes both the macro-level aspects, such as organizational culture, as well as more tactical approaches, such as human resources policies and hiring practices

- Technology Exploitation: Looking for ways to leverage new and advancing technologies to drive performance outcomes. This can include both technology for the sake of internal operations as well as differentiated technology to deliver services to the market

Each of these three focuses should already be present in any organization that is operating with any degree of stability. While the depth and breadth may vary depending upon the organization's size and industry, every organization has processes, every organization has organizational and human capital that must be effectively managed, and every organization leverages some kind of technology to some degree. If an organization does not take all of these into account, the risk of strategic misalignment becomes extremely high. An examination of the quotes in Table 3 provides perspective on how top-performing organizations are undertaking these efforts.

Table 3: Execution Approach Quotes

Focus	Sample Quotes from Study
Operational Performance	*Review facilities in order to optimize production. Review production processes to identify de-bottle necking opportunities. Review product offerings to enhance.*
	Just as the strategy does not change, neither do the capabilities, but we are always looking to add to their level.
	Get to root cause of capability, and how it could be utilized to build strengths and address weaknesses
Organizational Effectiveness	*We core capabilities are centered around employing the best people in each market place to meet the needs of our clients.*
	In our industry, you are only as good as your people.
	We look at the best people based on core competencies to perform according to expectations.
Technology Exploitation	*Since technology is the heart of the business, it is unquestioningly at the heart of our strategy formulation.*
	Developing the core technologies of our products is the heart of the strategy development process.

These processes are not mutually exclusive and should never be considered in a vacuum from each other. For example, looking at the Operational Performance and Technology Exploitation without considering how the people in the organization will use these capabilities (i.e., Organizational Effectiveness) significantly reduces the likelihood of the organization accomplishing its goals. Looking at the issues in total, however, allows the organization to take a full picture of how its capabilities contribute to its success.

This is similar to the systems thinking approach recommended by Senge (2006), and it is not uncommon to find that successful execution in one area contributing to success in another. A prime example of this is the earlier discussion of Walmart, which uses a Technology Exploitation approach to allow it to it to focus on Operational Excellence (Hamel

& Prahalad, 1994; Kim & Mauborgne, 1999; Scheraga, 2004). This in turn enables the associates on the sales floor (i.e., Organizational Effectiveness) to have the resources necessary to more effectively meet customers' needs.

How customers are integrated into these strategic planning efforts is the focus of the next chapter.

8: Applying Customer Information in the STS

With the rise of the educated consumer and increased competition for a shrinking share of the consumers' wallet, it is becoming more important for organizations to integrate customer considerations into their strategy processes. As discussed in chapter 5, the old assumption that the world will beat a path to your door just because you have a better mousetrap is no longer valid. Organizations must also make sure that customers know about their mousetrap, as well as make sure that customers see the mousetrap as worth any premium the organization puts on it for being better than the other options. Moreover, the quality of service provided in delivery of that mousetrap must meet or exceed the customers' expectations. In short, an organization better be thinking about the customer from the start.

So how do top-performing organizations integrate customer considerations into their strategy efforts? Based upon the feedback from the organizations that participated in this study, it appears that these activities tend to fit into three primary categories: Customer Insights, Market Insights, and Service Orientation.

Some people might see those categorizations and question why Customer and Market insights are separate, since the market is by definition a collection of customers. A valid question, but for sake of analysis, it is important to remember that Customer Insights are the microlevel considerations, while Market Insights are the macrolevel considerations. Each requires different data points and should be considered separately for strategic analysis activities. After the analysis, the resulting insights are combined to drive decisions about the organization's Service Orientation. The interactions between these elements are illustrated in Figure 6.

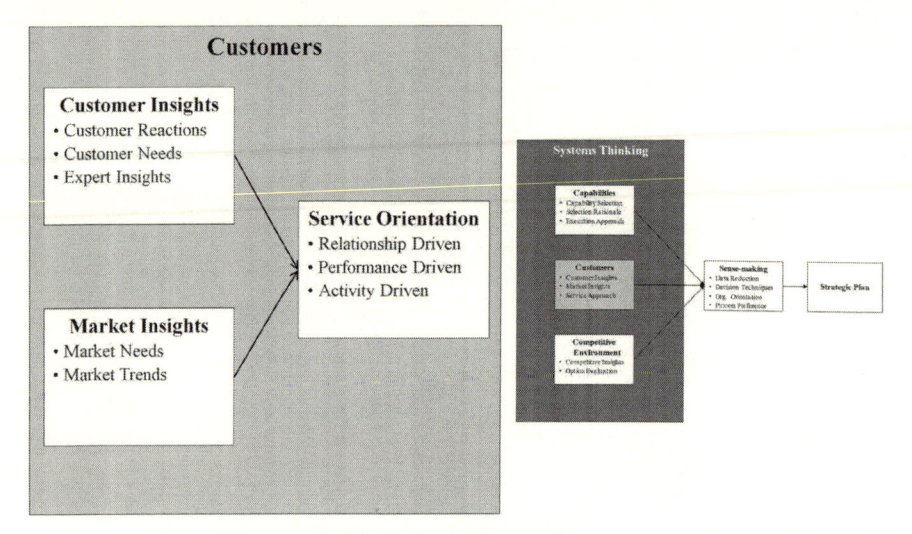

Figure 6. STS Customers Component

Customer Insights tend to be about understanding those customers who use and/or consume the products or services offered by the organization. Insights are focused toward individual consumers, and are concerned with driving those individuals toward particular transactions. To be clear, the term *individual* here refers to a single customer entity (e.g., person or organization) that will be making a purchase decision and engaging in the transaction. Understanding their insights is about determining how the organization should react to the customers' needs, and endeavoring to convince those individual customers that the organization is the best option to meet those needs. Typically these Customer Insights efforts integrate three types of data:

- Customer Reactions: Data about customers' behaviors and perceptions as a result of the actions the organization takes to try to serve them. – i.e., How the customer reacts to the organization and its efforts to meet their needs

- Customer Needs: Data about what the customers may need or want currently or at some time in the future, and what actions the organization may take to meet those needs. – i.e., This data drives how the organization reacts to its perceptions of the customers' needs

- Expert Insights: Input from people from within or outside of the organization who have some specialized knowledge about the customer base that may not be readily available to those individuals directly involved in the strategic planning process

Another central consideration when looking at Customer Insights is that these activities are focused on the direct relationship between the customer and the organization. It is important to note that these considerations are not just limited to commercial organizations whose goal is some kind of purchase activity. For a not-for-profit, the goal would be consider how the organization interacts directly with the population that is being served, to meet the needs of the members of that population. Governmental organizations would have a similar focus on their constituents and stakeholders.

Regardless of the transaction/interaction type, this is the part of the strategy in which the organization engages directly with the end user of its products and/or services. A review of the feedback from the participants in this study helps illustrate how this kind of information can be applied.

Table 4: Customer Insights Quotes

Data Type	Sample Quotes from Study
Customer Reactions	*Review customer satisfaction feedback to identify needed changes. Monitor weekly sales reports to identify missed opportunities. Review on-time delivery and quality statistics to identify opportunities.*
Customer Needs	*Identification of customer needs and our reaction to them is central to our success. Implementation of our strategy requires frequent contact with customers, and that contact enables us to react quickly to their needs. Also, frequent contact permits us to gauge the effectiveness of our response, and fine-tune it if need be.*
	We look both internally and externally. We look at our service and product mix and our customers' changing needs.
	Customer requirements are focused on closely, however this is by a natural understanding of the importance of this activity, rather than as a stated company requirement to 'focus on the customer'.
Expert Insights	*Product Managers are the customer experts in our organization. Products are defined based on customer and channel needs.*
	Rather than rely on a "marketing" or "sales" organization for business development, every line organization owns the responsibility to develop new customers and new business. The objective is to connect performing organizations directly to their customers thereby shortening the customer satisfaction communication link.
	We created a Chief Customer Officer position about 5 years ago. The person in this position is expected to integrate customer knowledge into the strategic planning process.

There is often confusion about where the line gets drawn between marketing and sales. While there have been attempts in both the applied and academic business literature to define a clear delineation between the two, the functional differentiations can vary greatly from organization to organization. It is not unusual for this differentiation to be driven by organizational politics as much as anything else.

That being said, reviewing and comparing all of those definitions here would not be prudent. What is prudent is putting a stake in the ground and saying that for this discussion, while Customer Insights are more focused on the individual customers and the transactions with them, Market Insights look more at the future and potentially unanticipated needs of the marketplace. In the same way that Customer Insights are about reacting to the customers' needs, marketing insights are about proactively anticipating what those needs may become. To do this, the market insights approach incorporates two categories of information:

- Market Needs: Data about the current state of the marketplace that may reveal needs of current and potential market segments that the organization could align itself to meet

- Market Trends: Data that enables understanding the direction and future position of the market so that the organization can anticipate changes that may need to be made to achieve advantage based on those shifts

When considering the current and future state of the market, the question of what to do with the data in order to gain the appropriate insights is always a tricky one. There is no shortage of analytical approaches and techniques that marketers use. Some are very sophisticated, such as multivariate regression analysis and customer profiling, while others are much simpler like the intuitive synthesis and experiential judgment type approaches discussed in chapter 6.

The decision points concerning what techniques to apply are often a function of what techniques the people in the marketing department are most familiar with, as well as what resources they have available. Not surprisingly the larger and more resourced the organization, the more sophisticated their approaches. This is true whether the organization is considering the current state of the market (i.e., Market Needs) or trying to predict the future state (i.e., Market Trends). As can be seen from the quotes in Table 5, it appears that the most important aspect of this phase is being willing to listen to what that data is saying and being open to the insights it provides.

Table 5: Marketing Insights Quotes

Categories	Sample Quotes from Study
Market Needs	*We constantly review the marketplace since we provide a differentiated service product in our market. We need to always be cognizant of the competition and the degree of a premium the customer is willing to pay for our services and not be sensitive to that "value" premium.*
	We conduct market research and spend time with Key Opinion Leaders (KOLs) in an attempt to identify unmet needs in the market. We are not inclined to force fit something we are capable of doing into our development plans without having a strong view of the market potential.
Market Trends	*Market research and customer feedback is an important component of our strategy development process. We talk to our customers continuously and keep a very close watch on our competition. Early identification of trends and innovations is also key.*
	We are focused on what our competition has and is likely to develop, however we tend to put more time and energy into determining how to address the needs of the market that we can uniquely address.

Of course all the Customer and Market Insights in the world are useless unless the organization decides to take some action based on them. Those decisions drive what Service Orientation the organization will adopt. The term Service Orientation here is consistent with previous definitions that look at the collection of dynamics that allow an organization to effectively manage their customers (Bowen, Siehl, & Schneider, 1989; Hogan, Hogan, & Busch, 1984). The difference is that this discussion looks at Service Orientation as an organizational-level issue rather than an individual-level issue.

Some may argue that looking at Service Orientation at the organizational level doesn't make much sense, given that it is often the individual interaction with the customer that most directly informs that customer's experience (Baskin, 2008). While that is true, it has already been established that organizations and the people in them tend to evolve in the direction of where they focus their energy (Cooperrider & Sekerka, 2003). So if the organization as a whole does not have the right Service Orientation , there is no reason to expect that the individuals in that organization will display the desired Service Orientation. Thus, establishing the right service orientation at the organizational level before attempting to drive it down to the individual level is critical.

The organizations that participated in this study tended to describe their Service Orientations in ways that could be classified into one or more of three categories:

- Relationship Driven: Aligning customer-facing activities around how the organization interacts with and relates to its customers. Includes communication, service levels, and direct interaction levels

- Performance Driven: Aligning customer-facing activities around outcome metrics associated with customer activities, and using those metrics as a primary tool to try to improve those activities

- Activity Driven: Selecting particular activities to focus on based upon customer needs, and driving the organization's strategy and activities based on those decisions

It is extremely rare for an organization's Service Orientation to focus on just one category. That, of course, begs the question: why are there three categories here? The answer comes down to a determination of priority—what will be the primary, secondary, and tertiary focuses of the organization.

Relationship Driven activities deal with the connections, affiliations, and rapport that a customer feels with the organization. In other words, is there a bond between the customer and the organization? Performance Driven activities are focused on how the quality of an organization's relationships compares to those of alternatives in the marketplace. These outcomes are measured by things like the customer ratings versus competitors. Activity Driven actions are the processes that the organization puts in place to drive the Relationship and Performance Outcomes.

While all of these issues are important, the organization must decide where it intends to focus first when it is developing its Service Orientation. An examination of the quotes in Table 6 provides further illustration.

Table 6: Service Orientation Quotes

Orientation Category	Sample Quotes from Study
Relationship Driven	Our senior sales and marketing people have frequent contact with key customers, and we also arrange meetings between our research people and research & development people at key customers to ensure that we understand their product/technology road-maps and they understand and accept ours.
Performance Driven	Best in class benchmarks; financial returns; market share; quality of services rendered; customer feedback; opinion of Wall Street; employee surveys.
Activity Driven	We are not all things to all people, but we are very good at providing services to a narrowly defined niche market. We don't differentiate on product (product is a commodity) but rather on service. Provide a high level of service is our core capability and we structure our organization to be able to provide such a high level of service.

As discussed in chapter 5, it is not hard to find examples of the application of these concepts in the literature. ExxonMobile NAM&R's and Harrah's both successfully integrated Customer and Market Insights into their strategy and refined their Service Orientations (Kaplan & Norton, 2001; Loveman, 2003; Sutton & Klein, 2003). In both cases, they leveraged understandings of Customer Needs and Market Needs to decide that they would be taking a more Relationship Driven approach that was enabled by an Activity Driven approach that focused on how they were going to treat specific customers in specific ways.

Of course, both of these examples involved an integration of a new customer perspective with an understanding of the organization's capabilities. In both of these cases, these insights allowed the organizations to out-perform and out-position their competitors, which is the focus of the next chapter.

9: The Competitive Environment in the STS

There is not much debate that focusing on the competitive environment is much more popular than the other strategy options. This may be a function of strategy's evolution from military thinking. It may reflect the success rate, at least in the short term, of business people with aggressive and competitive personalities. It may also be because most of the early discussions of business strategy were focused on competition and positioning in relation to the external environment (e.g., Porter). Or it could just be that many MBA programs still focus their strategy curricula on how the organization reacts to the competitive environment.

Regardless of the reasons, this approach remains the most fashionable despite mounting evidence that top-performing organizations take more holistic approaches that incorporate a broader range of insights. The evidence from this study suggests that the competitive environment should be considered only after the capabilities and customer components of the organization's strategy have been clearly defined.

Competition focused approaches look at how the organization positions itself in relationship to its environment (Porter, 1980), how it directly confronts competitors (Greenwald & Kahn, 2005), or how it avoids direct competition with rival organizations (Kim & Mauborgne, 2005). While the proponents of each of these approaches claim that they are unique, they are actually fundamentally the same, because reaction to the external environment is what is driving those decisions. How they respond may vary, but the drivers of those decisions are fundamentally the same.

Based upon the research for this book, those drivers appear to break down into two main areas. The first area is the Competitive Insights that are drawn from the available data on the various external forces that are impacting the organization. Many of the data points that are considered in this effort will be familiar to traditional business strategists.

The second area is the Option Evaluation process, during which the organization takes the Competitive Insights and analyzes them to determine how best to respond to forces in the environment. While there are any number of ways an organization could respond, the data suggests that those options tend to fall into three main categories.

Figure 7 illustrates the interaction between Competitive Insights and Option Evaluation.

Systems Thinking Strategy

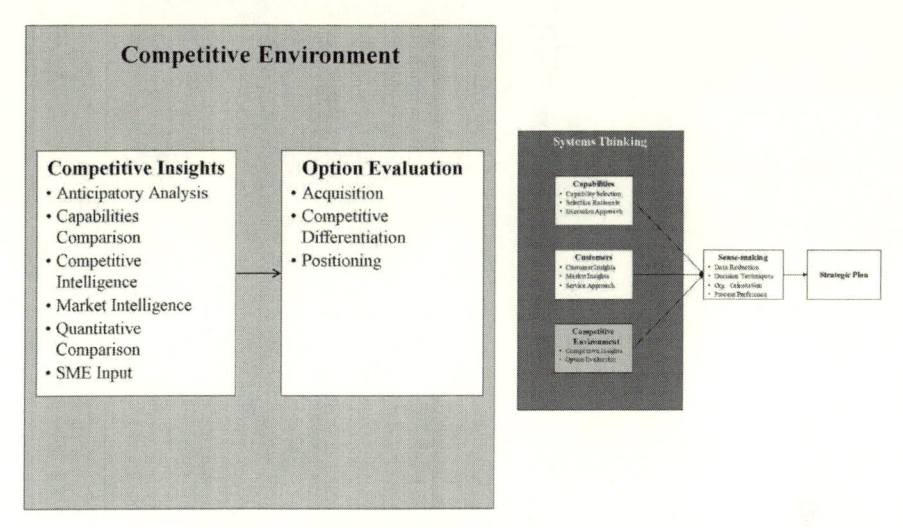

Figure 7. STS Competition Component

Many organizations tend to limit their strategy efforts to data points that are analogues of the Competitive Insights domain of this model. One of the reasons so many organizations are struggling may be this limitation of their strategic thinking to this one area and a corresponding lack of consideration for other critical inputs (i.e., capabilities and customers). If organizations did consider those other inputs, perhaps they would have a fuller view of their business ecosystem. This fuller view might allow for more informed business decisions, which could in turn help the organization be more successful.

That success would likely result from utilizing the broader view to inform decision making in relation to the Competitive Insights. Based upon the feedback from study participants, it appears that top-performing organizations make those Competitive Insights decisions by employing some mixture of six distinct processes:

- Anticipatory Analysis: Anticipating how the market may shift or change in the future, as well as competitors' reactions to those changes. Also includes anticipating competitors' reactions to the organization's own actions

- Capabilities Comparison: Comparing the organization to the competition based on the capabilities that can be leveraged for competitive advantage. An outward-focused capabilities analysis

- Competitive Intelligence: Actively gathering data about specific competitors so as to understand how their strategies, approaches, and offerings compare to those of the organization conducting the strategic planning process. May be an ongoing effort or limited to a specific period of time

- Market Intelligence: Gathering and analyzing data about the broader market and the forces that may be affecting it, rather than focusing on specific organizations that may be competing with the organization in question for resources, customers, or market share

- Quantitative Comparison: Comparing the organization to the competition based upon objective and quantifiable data. Includes peer-to-peer comparisons and comparison to competitive benchmarks

- SME Input: Leveraging insights and inputs from individuals who have direct knowledge of the competition and what they may be doing beyond that of most individuals who are involved in the strategic planning process

It should be noted that two of these categories listed here, Capabilities Comparison and Market Intelligence share some common characteristics with the two other domains already covered.

While this overlap may seem a bit confusing on the surface, the differentiation becomes clear when considering that the delineation is a matter of depth and focus. Typically, the depth of the analysis of these two areas at this phase the strategy development process is not nearly as deep as would be found when looking at capabilities or the market in the other two domains. Moreover, the focus is not on what the organization is best at itself, or how it can meet the needs of the market. The focus is on how the organization reacts to what its competitors are doing relative to these areas. This is another reason why competitive considerations should not come into play until after the capabilities and customers areas have been addressed.

The other four processes look at other kinds of data that the organization must consider. While the organization may not have access to data for all six processes, it should at least engage in the proper due diligence to determine the availability of that information. Table 7 helps illustrate this through quotes from the participants of this study.

Table 7: Competitive Insights Quotes

Processes	Sample Quotes from Study
Anticipatory Analysis	*Identifying emerging trends early and developing tactics and strategies to respond to these trends is extremely important to our business model. In response to changes in the competitive environment, we have effectively migrated along the supply chain away from manufacturing and production toward marketing, brand management and retail.*
Capabilities Comparison	*The business strategy is aimed at capitalizing on internal and organizational strengths. Those strengths are then analyzed in the context of the competitive environment and the results of that analysis is used to establish priorities for capital investment, research and development, etc. to strengthen the corporation's core capabilities.*

Processes	Sample Quotes from Study
Competitive Intelligence	*We operate in a "healthy state of paranoia"... constantly visiting the competition. At our meeting held every 4 weeks, each operations head must discuss what's going on with competition in their respective area.*
Market Intelligence	*We are focused on what our competition has and is likely to develop, however we tend to put more time and energy into determining how to address the needs of the market that we can uniquely address.*
Quantitative Comparison	*We use financial measures such as return on capital and EPS growth as compared to both the Fortune 500 and an industry peer group.*
SME Input	*Experts from each of our channels are brought in to discuss competition on a quarterly basis.*

Armed with the outcomes of these Competitive Insights, the organization must then make decisions about how it will, or will not, react to its external environment forces. This is essentially the positioning idea proposed in Porter's Five Forces model (1980).

The idea of positioning has always been tricky, and many people have had challenges understanding and conceptualizing it. Porter attempted address this concern in 2001 by identifying three positioning options that an organization could take, as discussed in chapter 3: variety-based, needs-based, or access-based. While these concepts are relevant in terms of identifying the destination options, there does not seem to be as much discussion about how organizations should get to those destinations.

Determining how an organization will move from its current state to its desired competitive position is termed here as Options Evaluation. While the decisions used to choose organizational direction are strategic, those decisions must consider the tactical nature of implementing those goals. In other words, the organization must carefully consider how well it is prepared to execute one of three choices:

- Acquisition: Attempting to gain competitive advantage by acquiring new entities that add capabilities, offerings, and/or customers rather than growing those advantages organically. Organic growth is addressed via development of capabilities

- Competitive Differentiation: Attempting to gain competitive advantage by focusing specifically on how the organization is different from its particular competitors

- Positioning: Determining the best place for the organization to place itself in the competitive market space. Can include placing itself against competitors it feels it can effectively compete with; placing itself in a space where it can partner with complementary organizations; or placing itself in an open space

While it is possible for organizations to apply all of these options to a varying degree within a single strategy, the simple truth is that many organizations do not. For example, some organizations choose to focus only on acquisitions, while others choose to focus only on how they position themselves. This narrow view often hinders their success. High-performing organizations, on the other hand, often take multiple options into account to varying degrees.

The quotes in Table 8 illustrate how the high-performing organizations that participated in this study approach these decisions.

Table 8: Options Evaluation Quotes

Choices	Sample Quotes from Study
Acquisition	*We are aware of our competencies and exploit those against our competition. Where we are weak, we often strengthen the organization through acquisition rather than internal development.*
Competitive Differentiation	*We constantly review the marketplace since we provide a differentiated service product in our LTL market. We need to always be cognizant of the competition and the degree of a premium the customer is willing to pay for our services and not be sensitive to that "value" premium.*
Positioning	*We are always interested in what our competitors are doing and look to learn as much as we can from the direction they are headed. We evaluate and assess issues that we see them address as they relate to our business. However, we have tended to go our own way and have often made decisions that are somewhat opposite of those made by our competitors.*

While a large number of participants provided feedback on how they approach Options Evaluation, most of the descriptions were fairly brief, and there was considerable overlap among the various themes. Interestingly, Positioning was discussed more often than either of the other possible approaches. There are several potential drivers for this.

The most obvious potential driver is the popularity of positioning could be the preponderance of writing on the topic by Porter and others. Another potential driver could be the phenomenon that Collis observed; organizations tend to spend much more time commiserating about where their organizations should end up (i.e., market position) than considering what strategic actions they will take to achieve their goals and turn their strategic visions into realities (2005).

One of the likely limitations that appears to be driving this gap between vision and action is that many organizations are simply unsure how to integrate a wide variety of data points into a single, coherent point of view that would enable them to take appropriate action. The process of integrating is the focus of the next chapter.

10: Making Sense in the STS

Once an organization has gathered the data about its capabilities, its customers, and its competitive environment, it must find the patterns and meaning in these mounds of information. This is the most difficult part, and the one where many organizations' strategy efforts fall short. An appropriate comparison could be gathering all the right ingredients for a cake, but forgetting to mix and bake them. There is no way that a proper cake will result. Hopefully this discussion will help organizations develop more fully baked strategies.

Sense-making is about taking the gathered information and making appropriate decisions based on that data. The value of considering sense-making as a discrete topic in the strategy discussion is that there is growing evidence that how an organization comes to these decisions has a direct link to its performance outcomes (Maitlis, 2005; Thomas et al., 1993). The more formalized and structured the process, the greater the likelihood of a beneficial outcome. More casual and/or informal approaches can be haphazard. This can significantly increase the risk of the organization making an inappropriate decision. A key contributor to properly executing any process is having a good model to follow.

Judging from the feedback received during this study, makings sense of the various inputs into the strategy process can be conceptualized into two sets of activities and two sets of influencers. The two sets of activities are Data Reduction and Decision Techniques. The two sets of influencers are Organizational Orientation and Process Preference. The relationships between the influencers and activities are cyclical, iterative, and mutually influential. The outcomes of one impact the other(s), and it may take several cycles to reach the final outcome. Figure 8 illustrates the model.

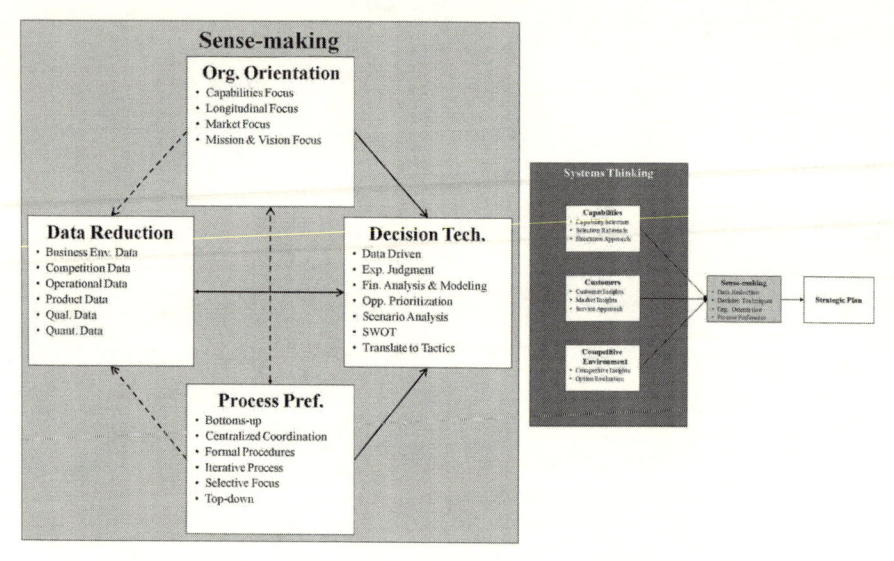

Figure 8. STS Sense-making Component

These activities are the *what*s of the sense-making process. Data Reduction is specifically focused on selecting and deselecting information from both internal and external sources that will be used in strategic decision making. This data is typically drawn from the outputs of the previously described efforts to incorporate the capabilities, customers and competitive environment parts of the strategy process. This data-gathering activity is similar to the Scanning variable that Thomas,

Clark, and Giola of Pennsylvania State University describe in their sense-making model (1993). The difference here is that the STS model is much more focused in its intent. Whereas other sense-making models look at general organizational activities, the STS model is focused specifically on strategic decisions. By focusing on strategy, the six most critical data types were identified:

- Business Environment Data: Data obtained through a macro view of the overall environment in which the organization operates. The goal is to understand how any changes to that environment do or could potentially impact the organization

- Competition Data: Data specifically focused around the behavior and/or offerings of other organizations that could compete against the organization for customers, resources, or market share

- Operational Data: Data focused on operational inputs and outputs over some period of time. Goal is to understand how the organization is driving toward desired outcomes

- Product Data: Data about the particular products the organization is bringing to the market and how they can be leveraged to better serve the market

- Qualitative Data: Data based on information and insights of a more subjective nature (i.e., cannot be directly quantified) that may be integrated into the strategic planning process

- Quantitative Data: Data based on information and insights of a more objective nature (i.e., can be directly quantified) that may be integrated into the strategic planning process

Using this data appears to be a two-step process. The first step is to gather as much data as is reasonable around capabilities, customers, and the competitive environment and then classify it based on the six categories above. While no organization that participated in this study reported a formal effort to include data across each of these particular six components, an examination of the feedback in total suggests that most successful organizations are considering data across a majority of these areas, even if they do not realize it. The recommendation at this point would be for an organization engaged in strategic efforts to strive to have enough data about capabilities, customers, and the competitive environment that that it can apply some insight to each of these six buckets.

Once this data is gathered, selection of which data points are the most relevant to the Decision Techniques phase begins. This is the reason for this activity to be termed Data Reduction.

The quotes in Table 9 illustrate the types of data actually utilized by the participants in this study.

Table 9: Data Reduction Quote

Types of Data	Sample Quotes from Study
Business Environment Data	*Strategy begins with a view of the market and a view on what customers are demanding of the industry and us. We project forward when we see emerging trends. We also look at our customer base from a global perspective, OE and after-market and commercial vs. military. We use industry research and our internal views to formulate our own view of where the industry is going.*
Competition Data	*We are always interested in what our competitors are doing and look to learn as much as we can from the direction they are headed. We evaluate and assess issues that we see them address as they relate to our business.*

Types of Data	Sample Quotes from Study
Operational Data	*Review facilities in order to optimize production. Review production processes to identify de-bottle necking opportunities. Review product offerings to enhance.*
Product Data	*We have historically focused on leveraging our core laser technology through new products and applications or distribution of products that are used in the same procedures as our laser-based products. As part of our strategic planning underway, we have begun to consider potentially disruptive technologies that may be a threat to our base business and partner with these potentially disruptive technologies.*
Qualitative Data	*Achievement of corporate objectives, under four measures of success—safe health and rewarding workplace; clean environment; supportive communities; and financial performance.*
Quantitative Data	*We attempt to focus on very summary level data and a few operating metrics for the existing business and industry wide valuation metrics, especially free cash flow for external growth.*

Once decisions are made about what kinds of data will be included in the strategy efforts, the organization must then decide how that data will be used. Decisions about Data Reduction, and selection of particular Decision Techniques appear to be mutually influential processes.

The outcomes of the Data Reduction efforts should drive the selection of particular Decision Techniques rather than preferences for particular Decision Techniques driving Data Reduction decisions. There is some suggestion, however, that some organizations let Decision Techniques drive Data Reduction efforts, but this is not recommended, as it is basically putting the cart before the horse.

There are also times when business leaders are called upon to make major decisions based on incomplete or imperfect data sets. While there may be times there this is unavoidable, it is also risky and presents the possibility for suboptimal decisions. In those cases where it cannot be avoided, the recommendation is to decide what techniques make sense for the organization and its market, and then determine how close they can get to those techniques based upon the available data. If the available data provides enough insight, go ahead and move forward. If there are significant data gaps, however, the organization should take the time to gather the necessary data. This approach will allow the organization and its leaders to make the most of a suboptimal situation.

Regardless of the quality and depth of the available data, it appears that the various tools and techniques used in these efforts can be grouped into seven approaches:

- Data-Driven: Approaches that are primarily focused on using available information (qualitative or quantitative) to understand how factors represented by that data could/do impact the organization

- Experiential Judgment: Approaches that are primarily based on experiences and intuition of individual(s) involved in the strategic planning process. Tends to leverage qualitative data more than quantitative data

- Financial Analysis and Modeling: Approaches that rely more on financial modeling and pro forma analysis (e.g., profitability, net income) as the primary catalysts for decision making

- Opportunity Prioritization: Approaches that focus on ranking potential opportunities based on some set of criteria, and then basing the selection of which opportunities the organization will pursue on those rankings

- Scenario Analysis: Approaches that focus on crafting various scenarios that describe potential outcomes based on some predefined and documented assumptions, and then basing decisions on an evaluation of the predicted outcomes of those possible scenarios

- SWOT: Approaches that focus on documenting the organization's Strengths, Weaknesses, Opportunities, and Threats, and then using that data to determine the best course of action. May also include approaches that are biased toward a purely strengths-based paradigm

- Translate to Tactics: Approaches that take broad strategic directives and then quickly move to the definition of tactics and the feasibility of those tactics to determine which options are most appropriate

Unlike the Data Reduction for which leading practice recommends beginning with data that cuts across all six components, it is extremely uncommon for an organization to use all seven Decision Technique approaches in a single effort. Most organizations typically utilize two to three of the approaches at any given time.

Interestingly, while many organizations incorporate some sort of financial modeling and analysis in this phase, not all do so. Those that do not utilize financial data appear to make the omission consciously in an effort to take a more longitudinal approach. While logic would suggest that some sort of investment analysis should occur at some point, it appears that the investment analysis is a secondary effort to validate decisions made on other grounds, rather than the primary driver of the decision process.

The Experiential Judgment or "trust your gut" technique is one of the most popular, but also one of the most risky of the decision techniques within the strategy domain. While it is quick and appears to be efficient, it also brings the potential for human error into the process. So why would such an approach appear in the STS model? While the more data-based approaches are great for eliminating options that definitely do not make sense, there may be times where two or more options seem to be equally viable based on the available data. Or there may be times when the approach that seems most attractive also requires significantly more investment than other viable options. In such cases, Experiential Judgment does appear to be an appropriate tiebreaker. However, these final selection scenarios are the only times where Experiential Judgment should be used.

The quotes in Table 10 illustrate how the participants in this study have applied the six Decision Techniques.

Table 10: Decision Technique Quotes

Techniques	Sample Quotes from Study
Data-Driven	*We try to make everything as fact-based as possible, so all premises, assumptions, etc. are typically supported by analysis.*
Experiential Judgment	*Overall, our organization lacks some of the basic data it needs to understand competitive strategies and tactics. Rather, they rely on professional experience and exposure to guide their decision making.*
Financial Analysis and Modeling	*Set objectives for the manufacturing and marketing processes. For example, detailed cost and inflation analysis, production capacity for new product activity is reviewed and built into planning process.*
Opportunity Prioritization	*We prioritize issues and only worry about analyzing top 2–3 uncertainties … which typically make up 90% of the value questions.*

Techniques	Sample Quotes from Study
Scenario Analysis	*Burden is placed on functional group leaders to distill various sources of information into actionable recommendation and also provide a contrasting case (what if we are wrong ...)*
SWOT	*We go through an assessment of strengths, weaknesses, opportunities and threats. We look to drive strategy to capitalize on market growth, acquisitions, new products, sales growth, profitability, etc.*
Translate to Tactics	*Definition of strategic vision by senior officers. Operating units develop plans to support that vision (Competing for corporate investments). Corporate develops plans to implement vision and optimize business units' plans. (Decides where to invest the money).*

These various techniques are similar to the Interpretation and Action phases of Thomas, Clark and Giola's sense-making model (1993), but again that model appears to be looking more at broad cognitive processes within an organization rather than understanding how the organization drives strategic outcomes.

Also of note is that the techniques described in the STS model could be used to varying degrees during different parts of the strategy formulation process. For example, Opportunity Prioritization and SWOT analysis are usually more appropriate early in the process, while the Financial Analysis and Modeling and Translate to Tactics activities tend to occur much later on.

An organization's decisions about which techniques to use and when their use would be most appropriate appeared to be a function of the organization's Organizational Orientation and Process Preference. Organizational Orientation is a critical consideration in deciding what data to use (i.e., Data Reduction) and how that data will be analyzed (i.e., Decision Techniques). It is so important because it informs how the organization sees itself and its environment, and how it wants to be viewed by others. This dynamic is similar to the way psychologists define personality, in that it drives the mental models that the organization uses to understand how it fits into the broader world. These mental models are key drivers of how the organization reacts to its ecosystem. They drive not only how the organization makes sense of the world, but also how it chooses to take action. In the case of strategy, these models tend to drive four distinct focuses:

- Capabilities Focus: Focusing primarily on the organization's internal capabilities and allowing that perspective to significantly impact the assumptions and decisions of the strategic planning process

- Longitudinal Focus: Taking a multiyear view of the organization that both integrates where the organization has been (i.e., historical performance) and where it wants to be over the next several years (e.g., 3–5 years) and allowing that perspective to significantly impact the assumptions and decisions of the strategic planning process

- Market Focused: Maintaining awareness of external market changes and potential evolving trends, and allowing that perspective to significantly impact the assumptions and decisions of the strategic planning process

- Mission & Vision Focus: Aligning strategic planning efforts around the organization's organization's mission and vision (i.e., why the organization exists) and allowing that perspective to significantly impact the assumptions and decisions in the strategic planning process

While some organizations choose to embrace only one focus, there are several scenarios where combinations of these focuses may complement each other. There are others where such combinations may conflict. For example, it is not uncommon to see an organization have a Mission & Vision Focus while simultaneously being longitudinally Focused. Trying to be Longitudinally Focused and Market Focused at the same time, however, typically does not work, as one focus requires the organization to be quickly responsive to changes in the market, while the other requires the ability to resist the urge to react to such influences.

Table 11 provides illustrations of how the organizations that participated in this study applied and integrated these focuses.

Table 11: Organizational Orientation Quotes

Focuses	Sample Quotes from Study
Capabilities Focus	*Understanding our core capabilities is critical to ensuring that we emphasize the skills/traits that will enable us to win in the marketplace. Building a strategy to compete on capabilities that are not currently resident in the company would require time, investment, and reduce probability of success.*
Longitudinal Focus	*Three year plans are developed annually by each individual business unit and submitted to executive management with a recommendation to Grow, Maintain or Exit. Three year plans include financial projections, market size and share, competitor evaluations, threats and opportunities, etc. Overall corporate strategy, capital resource allocation and acquisitions and divestitures are determined by executive management.*
Market Focused	*Our business changes quickly. We tend to let strategies evolve and make relatively quick decisions based on significant data provided to us.*
Mission & Vision Focus	*We are quite deliberative on the broad issues so that decisions are completely consistent with our mission statement. Accordingly, our business decisions tend to stay very close to our core values and competencies.*

While the Organizational Orientation is about what mental models the organization is using, the Process Preference is about how the organization chooses to get things done. These are not just the strategy activities, but the day-to-day actions required to execute that strategy and keep the organization functional.

While I did say early on that this book was not going to study the implementation of strategy, using a systems thinking approach does require that the organization's typical operating patterns be considered as part of strategic planning efforts. This consideration is important because some strategies simply will not work with some Process Preferences. For example, an organization that has a strong Formalized Procedures preference may have a hard time implementing a strategy that calls for more creativity and agility. If an organization has a process preference for a democratic style of management, taking a more Bottoms-Up approach may be the best option. The organization must carefully consider its preferences before any plans are finalized.

Process Preferences can be conceptualized into six categories:

- Bottoms-Up: Driving the strategic planning process by developing goals, objectives, and plans at the operating units and then integrating those plans into larger overall plans that then drive the larger organization

- Centralized Coordination: Management of strategic planning activities by a dedicated functional unit or group of resources that exist as an established, ongoing entity rather than an ad hoc group that exists for a finite period of time, and may or may not include the same individuals at a later date

- Formal Procedures: Management of the strategy formulation process through formal and prescriptive procedures to develop those plans. May include prescribed, repeatable steps, a predetermined format for strategic planning output, and/or establishment of a specific time and/or place where strategic issues are discussed and plans developed

- Iterative Process: Management of the strategy formulation process through multiple rounds of review and revision by a wide variety of stakeholders and subject matter experts

- Selective Focus: Processes that keep the organization focused on particular area(s) that are of critical importance to their business during analysis efforts. Objective is to not lose sight of what is important to maintaining organizational success

- Top-Down: Driving the strategic planning process by having senior leaders within the organization (e.g., CEO, board of directors, senior management team) come to agreement about the organization's goals and objectives, then promulgating those goals and objectives to the rest of the organization

Individual organization's Process Preferences aside, it should not be surprising that some of these approaches complement each other while others conflict. For example, it is all but impossible for an organization to have both a Top-Down and a Bottoms-Up preference at the same time. There are some organizations that might claim they do, in an effort to try to make the staff feel more engaged, but the truth is that the preference is usually for one or the other.

By the same token, it is all but impossible to have Centralized Coordination without Formalized Procedures. Those two focuses are only separated here because it is possible to have Formalized Procedures without Centralized Coordination. Some might even argue that a decentralized approach without formalization is extremely risky, but that discussion is best left for another time. The point of all this is that unless an organization is honest with itself about its true preference(s), and incorporate those considerations into its strategy processes, it runs the risk of not being successful.

Table 12 provides examples of how the organizations that participated in this study have taken preferences into account.

Table 12: Process Preference Quotes

Preference	Sample Quotes from Study
Bottoms-Up	*Business units develop their plans and review in a presentation with management that takes about 4 hours. Enterprise strategy is developed after having seen the individual business unit plans.*
Centralized Coordination	*A central strategy function coordinates the data gathering from the operations and the functions, synthesizes, analyzes and draws conclusions.*
Formal Procedures	*We have formal value creation methodology that we use to develop our business unit and functional strategies—to that end; much of our data is driven by expectations regarding overall market and historical performance. However, we lack some of customer, consumer, and competitive data to sufficiently inform our decision making processes. As a result, we default to our operational knowledge (how does cost impact the plant) to make most of our decisions.*
Iterative Process	*Information is presented to senior management team, who will often send the teams back to refine the information so that it may be optimized between the teams and cohesive for the consolidated company. It is a reiterative process.*
Selective Focus	*We tend to rely on a few sources that we believe are relevant to our specific business, and we do not subscribe to every late and great market survey or study.*

Preference	Sample Quotes from Study
Top-Down	*Corporate management (CEO/COO) establishes high level quantitative and qualitative goals and objectives for the planning period(s). Organizational management formulates strategic plans for their respective organizations, aimed at achieving the corporate goals, briefs those plans to management, and after a process of negotiation and reconciliation the plans are implemented.*

Centralized Coordination, Formal Procedures, Iterative Processes, and Selective Focus all appear to be nonmutually exclusive focuses, each resting along their own continuums. As such the integration of these four preferences can vary from organization to organization.

As discussed earlier, however, Bottoms-Up and Top-Down approaches are mutually exclusive ends of the same continuum. This begs the question of why they are separate categories in this analysis. The answer lies in the fluidity versus the rigidity of these two preferences. While the centralization or formality of an organization may change over time, the degree to which an organization has a Bottoms-Up or a Top-Down approach tends to remain constant unless there is some major event (e.g., acquisition or merger) that changes the character of that organization. This is the primary reason why these two approaches warrant separate classifications. It should be noted, however, that the Top-Down approach appears to be the more common among the responses from participants in this study, and is more consistent with the descriptions in the literature at large.

Now the data about capabilities, customers, and the competitive environment has been gathered, and the decisions have been made about how the organization will make sense of these mounds of data; the question becomes what should the organization do next?

The answer to that question is actually quite simple. Make the plan, execute the plan, and then measure the results. If the results aren't meeting expectations, investigate why and adjust as appropriate. There are lots of proven approaches that work well when the strategic plan is right.

The challenge up to this point, however, has been that the approaches used for strategic planning efforts have not always taken the organization's full ecosystem into account. This deficiency risks the organization missing some critical piece of information. By defining the types of data that need to be included in the strategy effort and how to make sense of them, the Systems Thinking Strategy model mitigates that risk.

11: Lessons Learned

One of those useful tasks that any individual or organization can undertake is to review an activity they have completed and identify their lessons learned. There are several such lessons that can be gleaned from this book.

The first is that that top-performing organizations do take multidimensional views of their organizations and the ecosystems in which they exist. They use mental models to consider what the organization can do, who they are trying to serve, and what environmental actors might inhibit their ability to serve those constituents. Most importantly, they make the effort to be sure they are considering all the impacting issues. In other words, they look at their world through a systems thinking lens.

This claim is supported both by the published literature and by feedback from top-performing organizations. Moreover, statistical analysis of the data suggests the strength of these patterns would occur by random chance less than 0.1% of the time. The higher standard for statistical significance in the behavioral sciences is less than 1% of the time. In other words, these patterns are extremely statistically significant, and have more than enough statistical support to quiet the challenges of most skeptics.

The second lesson from this study relates to performance. Will adopting the STS model help an organization improve its performance metrics? While this study did not follow a classical experimental design model that specifically tracked performance and improvement or organizations using the STS model outcomes, those variables were controlled for by limiting participants to top-performing organizations. This kind of purposeful selection to make such a case is an accepted approach in research. The success of these organizations and the degree to which their activities align to the described model supports the claim that such an approach appears to contribute to performance. To double check this assertion, participants were asked how much their strategies impacted their organizations' performance. They overwhelmingly reported that their strategies had a positive impact on their organizations' performance. The combination of these two insights suggests that the utilization of an STS like model would have a positive impact on an organization's performance.

There is also evidence that capabilities, customers, and the competitive environment are the primary categorizations of data that should be used. These categorizations are useful because they clearly describe the assumptions and generalizations that managers need to take into account when incorporating fuller perspectives into their strategy formulation activities. Having these understandings does not, however, provide much benefit unless the organization can make sense of that information so appropriate business decisions can be made.

The final lesson learned is about how organizations go about these sense-making activities. In simplest terms, the sense-making process is about understanding how organizations decide what data they will include in and exclude from their strategy formulation processes, and then what techniques they will use to manipulate that data to come to decisions. The selection of data and techniques is typically driven by both the organizational and tactical orientations of the organization in question.

The most important question of this whole effort is how does an organization apply the concepts that have been presented here? To begin to answer that question, let's level set that every organization has capabilities, every organization has customers, and every organization operates within a competitive environment. Customers may be internal or external, or they may be called something like stakeholder or constituents or even beneficiaries, but the simple fact is that every organization has them. Some organizations may say they do not have direct competition, but any time a customer has the option to not use your particular services or there is another organization competing for resources, that environment is by definition competitive. Any organization that wants to be successful should assume that all three elements are present and drive their strategies accordingly.

Considering these lessons learned, how can these insights be applied to drive performance? For starters, they can be applied to develop a deep understanding of the relevant data points described in the components of this model. This may sound like a blatant oversimplification of a robust process, but as we all know from studying Occam's razor, often the simplest solution is best.

For capabilities, an organization should take a hard look at strengths, needs, and how those align with the organization's efforts to differentiate. The organization should take an equally hard look at customer insights and market insights. Comparison with the organization's competitive insights will yield an evaluation of the organization's options for dealing with any challenges that may be faced in the environment. The organization can then engage in data reduction, and make the appropriate choices about what is best for the organization. Taking these simple steps will lead to a more comprehensive and robust strategy that will set the organization on the right path to drive best performance.

List of Figures

Figure 1. Porter's Five Forces Model 15

Figure 2. Illustration of Hamel and Prahalad's Core Competency-Based Approach 25

Figure 3. Systems Thinking Strategy 40

Figure 4. Detailed Systems Thinking Strategy 44

Figure 5. STS Capabilities Component 47

Figure 6. STS Customers Component 56

Figure 7. STS Competition Component 67

Figure 8. STS Sense-making Component 76

Figure 9. Research Model 99

Figure 10. Questionnaire Response Histogram 110

List of Tables

Table 1: Capabilities Selection Quotes. 49

Table 2: Rationale Quotes 51

Table 3: Execution Approach Quotes 53

Table 4: Customer Insights Quotes 58

Table 5: Marketing Insights Quotes. 60

Table 6: Service Orientation Quotes 63

Table 7: Competitive Insights Quotes 69

Table 8: Options Evaluation Quotes 72

Table 9: Data Reduction Quote. 78

Table 10: Decision Technique Quotes 82

Table 11: Organizational Orientation Quotes 85

Table 12: Process Preference Quotes 88

Table 13: Data Collection Response Rates. 106

Table 14: Overall Demographic Comparisons. 107

Table 15: Data to Hypothesis Linkage. 109

Table 16: Means and Standard Deviations. 111

Table 17: Chi-Squared Calculations 113

Research Notes

This book is based upon a doctoral dissertation study that used the following research question:

Do organizations that take an approach to strategy formulation that is consistent with a model based on a systems thinking perspective perform better than the overall market?

This question was answered by gathering feedback from top-performing organizations about their strategy processes. A questionnaire was distributed to the identified organizations and their responses were analyzed. Figure 9 illustrates this approach.

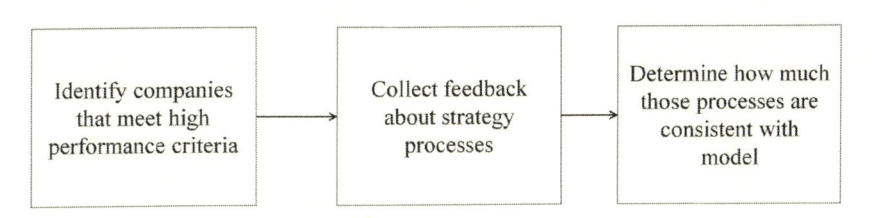

Identify companies that meet high performance criteria	→	Collect feedback about strategy processes	→	Determine how much those processes are consistent with model

Figure 9. Research Model

Participant Identification
Potential participants were identified based on their performance along the metrics of stock performance over a set period of time, and gross

sales. These variables were chosen because they have commonly agreed definitions of performance, and because this data is readily available for publicly traded companies. This kind of purposeful selection of participants based on existing data is a well-established technique in the management sciences and has been used in works such as *Good to Great* and *Built to Last* (Collins, 2001; Collins & Porras, 2002), as well as Kaplan & Norton's *Balanced Scorecard* work (2001, 2004).

For top performers based on stock price, a data set that identified and ranked the 200 top-performing publicly traded companies in terms of total stock market returns between January 1, 2001, and December 31, 2005, was purchased from the Center for Research in Security Prices (CRSP) at the University of Chicago. The data set included the name of each company, its total return ranking, stock trading symbol, and Standard Industry Classification (SIC) code. Additional information was also readily available from various websites, such as *The Wall Street Journal* (www.wsj.com) and *Fortune* magazine (www.fortune.com).

Top performers in terms of gross sales were identified based on their rankings in the most recent Fortune 500 prior to the start of data collection. The decision to use this list was based upon it being easily obtainable from the www.fortune.com website, and wide recognition that this list includes leading companies. The website lists company name, stock trading symbol, gross sales, and profits from the previous year. The list used for this study included sales through December 31, 2005. In addition, lists of names and e-mail addresses for executives in Fortune 500 companies can easily be purchased from several different sources. Purchasing names and contact information were consistent with several other studies that were reviewed as a part of this project (Panayides, 2004; Ramanujam, Venkatraman, & Camillus, 1986; Watson & Wooldridge, 2005).

Questionnaire Development

Since this project investigated a model that had not been previously studied, a custom questionnaire was developed. This was done by mapping the original version of the multi-dimensional strategy model (the term used for the STS model during the study) to the quantitative hypotheses for the project.

The quantitative hypotheses were as follows:

H_1: Organizations in the selected data set will report being deliberative about their strategy formulation processes more often than would be expected by chance alone

H_2: Organizations in the selected data set will report including competitors in their strategy formulation efforts more often than would be expected by chance alone

H_3: Organizations in the selected data set will report including capability type information in their strategy formulation process more often than would be expected by chance alone

H_4: Organizations in the selected data set will report including both capabilities and competitors as units of analysis in their strategy formulation process more often than would be expected by chance alone

H_5: Organizations in the selected data set will report including customers as a distinct unit of analysis in their strategy formulation processes more often than would be expected by chance alone

H_6: Organizations in the selected data set will report including customers and competitors in their strategy formulation processes more often than would be expected by chance alone

H_7: Organizations in the selected data set will report including both customers and capabilities in their strategy formulation processes more often than would be expected by chance alone

H_8: Organizations in the selected data set will report including customers, capabilities, and competitors in their strategy formulation processes more often than would be expected by chance alone

Based upon these mappings, a questionnaire was developed and distributed via the ZipSurvey application (www.zipsurvey.com). This questionnaire included the following sections:

- Section 1 – Identification Items: These section was used to determine which organization was reporting the data. This included questionnaire items 1–6
- Section 2 – Strategy Impact Items: This section addressed the concerns of researchers who report that business strategies are not perceived as impactful on organizational performance. This section includes one 5-point Likert scale item asking respondents to rate the perceived impactfulness of their strategy development efforts, and one open-ended item asking the respondents to describe the kinds of criteria that they used to classify themselves as performing well or not performing well. This section included questionnaire items 7 and 8
- Section 3 – Deliberativeness of the Strategy Process: This section included one 5-point Likert scale item asking the respondents to rate how deliberative their strategy formulation efforts are, as well as an open-ended item asking the respondents to describe the process they use. This section included questionnaire items 9 and 10, and is associated with H_1

- Section 4 – Use of Competitive Information: This section included one 5-point Likert scale item asking respondents to rate the degree to which they include information about competition and the environment in their strategy formulation processes, and an open-ended item asking them to describe the data elements they include in those efforts. This section included questionnaire items 11 and 12, and was associated with H_2, H_4, H_6, H_8, and Q_1
- Section 5 – Use of Capabilities Information: This section included one 5-point Likert scale item asking respondents to rate the degree to which they include information about capabilities in their strategy formulation processes, and an open-ended item asking them to describe what data elements they include in those efforts. This section included questionnaire items 13 and 14, and was associated with H_3, H_4, H_7, H_8, and Q_2
- Section 6 – Use of Customer Information: This section included one 5-point Likert scale item asking respondents to rate the degree to which they include information about customers and their needs in the organizations' strategy formulation processes, and an open-ended item asking the respondents to describe what data elements they include in those efforts. This section included questionnaire items 15 and 16, and was associated with H_5, H_6, H_7, H_8, and Q_3
- Section 7 – Sense-making: This section included one open-ended item that asked respondents to describe the processes they use to understand and utilize the various kinds of data during their organizations' strategy formulation processes. This section included questionnaire item 17 and was associated with Q_4

Data Collection

The data collection phase of this study had two sub-phases. The first sub-phase focused on collecting feedback from organizations that were identified by the CRSP as part of the 200 top-performing organizations between 2001 and 2005 (Top 200). The second sub-phase focused on collecting data from organizations that were part of the Fortune 500 for 2005 (Fortune 500).

Many of the Top 200 organizations were relatively small, and purchasing contact names and e-mail addresses, as was done with the Fortune 500 participants, was not feasible. Moreover, publicly available information from sources such as WSJ.com and Fortune.com often only listed investor relations e-mail contacts, rather than e-mail addresses of individuals who might be involved in the strategy formulation process.

What was listed in many cases, however, were general telephone numbers and the names of officers within the organization. Using this information, attempts were made to cold-call the Top 200 organizations and request to speak with either an individual with a title related to strategy formulation, or someone within the office of the chief financial officer (CFO). Anyone who agreed to participate was forwarded an e-mail that provided more details about the study and a link to the on-line questionnaire. Reminders were sent to individuals who indicated that they would participate, but who did not respond to the initial e-mail within approximately two weeks and four weeks after the initial e-mail requests.

Of the Top 200 organizations, 91 agreed to receive e-mail requests, 21 declined to participate, and 38 were determined to be not reachable. A total of 48 responses were received from this group; however, only 43 were determined to be usable. Usability determinations were based upon the respondent completing all Likert scale-based items on the questionnaire. The final usable response rate for the Top 200 sub-phase of the data collection effort was 26.5%.

Since names and e-mails for key individuals in Fortune 500 organizations could be purchased from third-party sources, the Fortune 500 sub-phase did not require any cold-calling. The purchased list was reviewed to eliminate contact information for any organization that was not publicly traded, and then to remove contact information for any individual who appeared to be inappropriate for this study (e.g., a vice president of accounting). Also, organizations for which contact information was not included in the purchased list were classified as unreachable.

The resulting list included contact information for 472 organizations, four of which were also part of the Top 200. Those four companies were not resolicited. E-mail requests to participate in the study, with a hyperlink to the questionnaire, were sent to contacts in 468 companies. The e-mail also included the offer of a complementary summary report of the findings of the study if a response was provided. Reminders were forwarded at two- and four-week intervals after the initial e-mail request.

After each round, e-mails that were returned as undeliverable were reviewed to determine which organizations should be classified as unreachable. A total of 171 organizations listed as part of the Fortune 500 were classified as unreachable during this study. Thirty organizations provided responses to the questionnaire, of which 23 were determined to be usable according to criteria consistent with those employed for the responses from the Top 200 organizations. The final usable response rate for the Fortune 500 sub-phase of the data collection effort was 7.7%. Combining the two sub-phases, the overall usable response rate for this effort was 14.4%. Table 13 details this information.

Table 13: Data Collection Response Rates

	Top 200	Fortune 500
Total Population	200	500
Not Publicly Traded	N/A	28
Duplicates from Top 200	N/A	4
Not-Reachable	<u>38</u>	<u>171</u>
Usable Sample	162	297
Total Responses	48	30
Usable Responses	43	23
Response Rate	26.5%	7.7%
Overall Response Rate		14.4%

Sample Representativeness

Sample representativeness helps determine the degree to which the results of a sample appear to be consistent with the overall population. Response rates and comparison to demographic characteristics are the two primary ways to determine representativeness.

The response rates for strategy-related studies in academic journals range from 14% to 34% (Harrington, Lemak, Reed, & Kendall, 2004; Panayides, 2004; Ramanujam et al., 1986; Watson & Wooldridge, 2005). While the 14.4% response rate for this study is on the low end of that continuum, it is within the accepted range. Based upon this, the data for this study does pass the response rate test for representativeness.

The two demographics that were used for this study were number of employees and total sales volume for 2005. Table 14 compares these data points between the total population and the responding population. It also identifies the percentage of each group that fell into each category. Table 14 also illustrates the differences between the total and responding populations on a category by category basis. Based upon this, it respondents for this study did not appear to be markedly different than the targeted population.

Table 14: Overall Demographic Comparisons

Total Employees

Total Count	Employees	Percent	Responded Count	Employees	Percent	Diff.
247	> 10000	53.81%	22	> 10000	29.73%	24.08%
47	5000 – 9999	10.24%	7	5000 – 9999	9.46%	0.78%
68	1000 – 4999	14.81%	17	1000 – 4999	22.97%	-8.16%
26	500 – 999	5.66%	8	500 – 999	10.81%	-5.15%
31	250 – 499	6.75%	8	250 – 499	10.81%	-4.06%
22	100 – 250	4.79%	8	100 – 250	10.81%	-6.02%
18	< 100	3.92%	4	< 100	5.41%	-1.48%
459			74			7.10%

Sales for 2005

Total Count	Sales	Percent	Responded Count	Sales	Percent	Diff.
46	> $25B	10.02%	5	> $25B	6.76%	3.27%
94	$10B - $25B	20.48%	7	$10B - $25B	9.46%	11.02%
185	$1B - $10B	40.31%	29	$1B - $10B	39.19%	1.12%
21	$500MM - $1B	4.58%	2	$500MM - $1B	2.70%	1.87%
28	$250MM - $499MM	6.10%	10	$250MM - $499MM	13.51%	-7.41%
41	$100M - $250M	8.93%	9	$100M - $250M	12.16%	-3.23%
22	$50M - $100M	4.79%	6	$50M - $100M	8.11%	-3.32%
22	< $50M	4.79%	6	< $50M	8.11%	-3.32%
459			74			4.32%

Quantitative Analysis & Results

The quantitative analysis phase focused on determining the degree to which the data supported the stated hypotheses. The first determination of support was made based on the directionality of the results. The second determination of support was based on an assessment of the likelihood that those results were more pronounced than could be expected by chance alone.

There were eight hypotheses associated with this study. Four of those hypotheses (H_1, H_2, H_3, and H_5) made predictions that could be assessed based on responses to individual questionnaire items. Each of those items was associated with a particular variable within the SPSS database that was used for the analysis. The four remaining hypotheses (H_4, H_6, H_7, and H_8) required that new variables be created by combining other feedback using the SPSS software's Compute functionality. These new variables were averages of the scores for the items associated with competitors, capabilities, and customers so as to determine the degree to which organizations incorporated more than one view into their strategy formulation activities. Table 15 illustrates the linkage of these hypotheses to the variables in the data set.

Table 15: Data to Hypothesis Linkage

Variable	Formula	Hypothesis
Impact	N/A	*N/A – Question included to assess participants perception of strategy's impact on their organization's performance*
Deliberative	N/A	H1: Organizations in the selected data-set will report being deliberative about their strategy formulation processes more often than would be expected by chance alone
Competition	N/A	H2: Organizations in the selected data-set will report including competitors in their strategy formulation efforts more often than would be expected by chance alone
Capabilities	N/A	H3: Organizations in the selected data-set will report including core competency type information in their strategy formulation process more often than would be expected by chance alone
Customers	N/A	H5: Organizations in the selected data-set will report including customers as a distinct unit of analysis in their strategy formulation processes more often than would be expected by chance alone
Comp_Cap	= (Competition + Capabilities)/2	H4: Organizations in the selected data-set will report including both capabilities and competitors as units of analysis in their strategy formulation process more often than would be expected by chance alone
Comp_Cust	=(Competition + Customers)/2	H6: Organizations in the selected data-set will report including customers and competitors in their strategy formulation processes more often than would be expected by chance alone
Cap_Cust	=(Capabilities + Customers)/2	H7: Organizations in the selected data-set will report including both customers and capabilities in their strategy formulation processes more often than would be expected by chance alone
Comp_Cap_Cust	=(Competition + Capabilities + Customers)/3	H8: Organizations in the selected data-set will report including customers, capabilities, and competitors in their strategy formulation processes more often than would be expected by chance alone

Once the data manipulation was complete, it was possible to perform appropriate analyses. The first analyses involved examining simple histograms for each of the five variables that were associated with a single item within the questionnaire. Figure 10 illustrates these results.

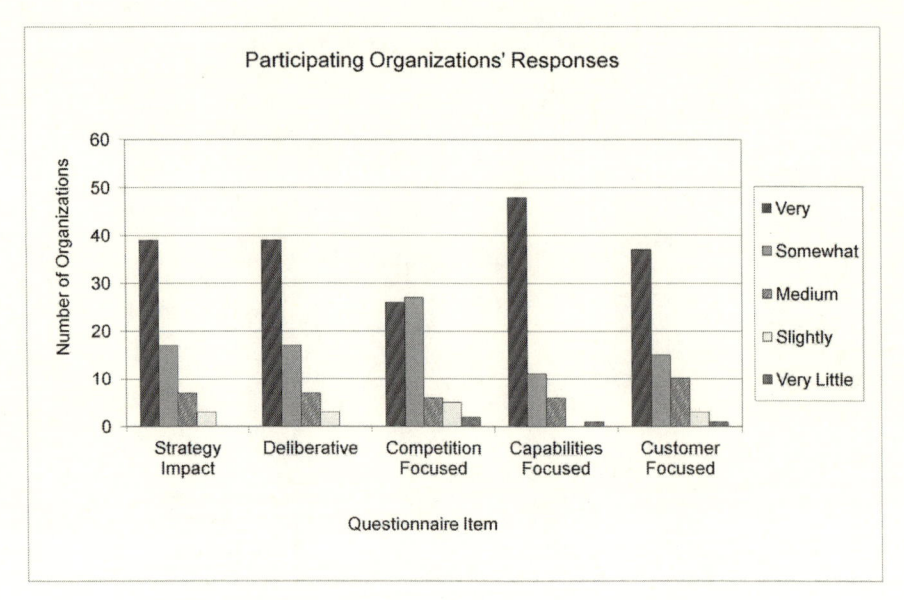

Figure 10. Questionnaire Response Histogram

The responses to the questionnaire trend toward the positive side of the response scales for each item. This trending is made even more apparent when the means and standard deviations for all items are examined, as they are in Table 16. With no single mean below 4.06, the assertion can be made that the positive trend in the data does tend to support the hypotheses that have been presented here.

Table 16: Means and Standard Deviations

Variable	Hypothesis	Mean	Std.	N
Impact	N/A – Question included to assess participants perception of strategy's impact on their organization's performance	4.39	0.86	66
Deliberative	H1: Organizations in the selected data-set will report being deliberative about their strategy formulation processes more often than would be expected by chance alone	4.06	1.15	66
Competition	H2: Organizations in the selected data-set will report including competitors in their strategy formulation efforts more often than would be expected by chance alone	4.06	1.04	66
Capabilities	H3: Organizations in the selected data-set will report including core competency type information in their strategy formulation process more often than would be expected by chance alone	4.59	0.78	66
Customers	H5: Organizations in the selected data-set will report including customers as a distinct unit of analysis in their strategy formulation processes more often than would be expected by chance alone	4.27	0.99	66
Comp_Cap	H4: Organizations in the selected data-set will report including both capabilities and competitors as units of analysis in their strategy formulation process more often than would be expected by chance alone	4.33	0.65	66
Comp_Cust	H6: Organizations in the selected data-set will report including customers and competitors in their strategy formulation processes more often than would be expected by chance alone	4.17	0.79	66
Cap_Cust	H7: Organizations in the selected data-set will report including both customers and capabilities in their strategy formulation processes more often than would be expected by chance alone	4.43	0.76	66
Comp_Cap_Cust	H8: Organizations in the selected data-set will report including customers, capabilities, and competitors in their strategy formulation processes more often than would be expected by chance alone	4.31	0.65	66

While the positive trend did appear to support the hypotheses, the statistical significance of those trends must also be tested. The chi-squared (χ^2) test was chosen due to its ability to assess the significance between expected and observed frequencies in a given distribution (Pophan & Sirotnik, 1992). The larger the resulting χ^2 for each difference, the greater the likelihood that the observed distribution is due to something other than chance. The SPSS χ^2 function was used to perform these calculations, with the expectation that chance alone would result in relatively even distribution of responses across each of the variables.

Table 17 displays each variable, its associated hypothesis, the resulting χ^2, the degrees of freedom (df) for each variable, and the statistical significance of the resulting χ^2 calculation. In simplest terms, *degrees of freedom* is an assessment of the number of possible variations within a given item (Pophan & Sirotnik, 1992). When performing the χ^2 calculation, the df is determined by the number of possible responses to an item minus one. Since each item in the questionnaire used a 5-point Likert scale, the df for each item was therefore equal to four. For items with df=4, a χ^2 equal to or greater than 18.465 would be considered significant at the .001 level. This would mean that such a distribution would be expected less than 0.1% of the time by chance alone.

Each of the eight items attached to a hypothesis had a χ^2 calculation of at least 32.04, meaning that they were all greater than the necessary threshold for retaining them at the .001 level. This is significantly more significant than the .01 level threshold normally found in academic research.

Table 17: Chi-Squared Calculations

Variable	Hypothesis	X^2	df	Sig.
Impact	N/A – Question included to assess participants perception of strategy's impact on their organization's performance	54.47	4	0.000
Deliberative	H1: Organizations in the selected data-set will report being deliberative about their strategy formulation processes more often than would be expected by chance alone	32.04	4	0.000
Competition	H2: Organizations in the selected data-set will report including competitors in their strategy formulation efforts more often than would be expected by chance alone	38.84	4	0.000
Capabilities	H3: Organizations in the selected data-set will report including core competency type information in their strategy formulation process more often than would be expected by chance alone	82.30	4	0.000
Customers	H5: Organizations in the selected data-set will report including customers as a distinct unit of analysis in their strategy formulation processes more often than would be expected by chance alone	52.63	4	0.000
Comp_Cap	H4: Organizations in the selected data-set will report including both capabilities and competitors as units of analysis in their strategy formulation process more often than would be expected by chance alone	73.77	4	0.000
Comp_Cust	H6: Organizations in the selected data-set will report including customers and competitors in their strategy formulation processes more often than would be expected by chance alone	74.58	4	0.000
Cap_Cust	H7: Organizations in the selected data-set will report including both customers and capabilities in their strategy formulation processes more often than would be expected by chance alone	54.41	4	0.000
Comp_Cap_Cust	H8: Organizations in the selected data-set will report including customers, capabilities, and competitors in their strategy formulation processes more often than would be expected by chance alone	85.78	4	0.000

Qualitative Analysis & Results

Since the all the hypotheses were retained, the focus of the qualitative analysis phase was to gain a deeper understanding of what was common across the strategy formulation processes of the responding organizations, so that these insights could be used to add depth to the model. To develop these understandings, the qualitative phase of research was guided by four questions of inquiry:

Q_1: What is common across the organizations in the selected data set relative to the use of competitor information in their strategy formulations efforts?

Q_2: What is common across the organizations in the selected data set relative to the use of capability information in their strategy formulation efforts?

Q_3: What is common across the organizations in the selected data set relative to the use of customer information in their strategy formulation efforts?

Q_4: What is common across the organizations in the selected data set relative to their efforts to engage in synthesis and sense-making during their strategy formulation efforts?

This phase involved assembling the comments from the open-ended items of the questionnaire into MS Word documents that could be uploaded in Atlas.ti for coding and analysis. Separate documents were assembled for comments related to capabilities, customers, and competitive environment, as well as sense-making. Each hermeneutic unit was analyzed according to the following five-step process.

- Pure Open Coding: Reviewed the text within each hermeneutic unit and coding each word or section of text in an approach consistent with Strauss and Corbin's micro-analysis recommendations (1998)
- First-Level Data Reduction: Reviewed the results of the previous step to identify those codes that should obviously be combined based upon differences such as misspellings or word order
- Second-Level Data Reduction: Reviewed the quotations associated with each coding label and then developed short definitions for each one. The resulting definitions for each code were then reviewed to identify those that seemed to be addressing the same phenomena, particularly in terms of skills, data, or perspectives used in that part of the strategy formulation process. Quotations for those codes were then reviewed, and

code labels that appeared to address the same phenomena were combined and renamed appropriately
- Axial Coding: Developed an understanding of how the various codes within each hermeneutic unit related to each other. The first step in this process was developing more robust definitions for the remaining codes. Codes that seemed to address related processes were grouped into domains. which are referred to as *code families* in Atlas.ti terminology. Once each domain was developed, graphical representations of how the various processes represented by the codes within the domain related to each other were developed
- Selective Coding: Crafted descriptions of the observed phenomena so that the processes could be better understood and the new insights incorporated into the model as appropriate

The outcomes of this effort are described in chapters 7–10.

References

Baskin, J. S. (2008). *Branding only works on cattle: The new way to get known (and drive your competitors crazy)*. New York, NY: Business Plus.

Bowen, D. E., Siehl, C., & Schneider, B. (1989). A framework for analyzing customer service orientations in manufacturing. *Academy of Management Review, 14*, 75–96.

Brown, J. (2007). *Leveraging an OD perspective to develop a new model of strategy formulation*. Lisle, IL: Benedictine University.

Carey, R. G., & Lloyd, R. C. (2001). *Measuring quality improvement in healthcare*. Milwaukee, WI: Quality Press.

Collins, J. (2001). *Good to great*. New York, NY: HarperBusiness.

Collins, J., & Porras, J. I. (2002). *Built to last*. New York, NY: Collins Business Essentials.

Collis, D. J. (2005). *Strategy: Create and implement the best strategy for your business*. Boston: Harvard Business School Press.

Collis, D. J., & Montgomery, C. A. (1995). Competing on resources: Strategy in the 1990s. *Harvard Business Review, 73*, 118-128.

Cooperrider, D. L., & Sekerka, L. E. (2003). Toward a theory of positive organizational change. In K. S. Cameron, J. E. Dutton, & R. E. Quinn (Eds.), *Positive organizational scholarship* (pp. 225–240). San Francisco, CA: Berrett-Koehler.

Cummings, S., & Angwin, D. (2004). The future shape of strategy: Lemmings or chimeras? *Academy of Management Executive, 18,* 21–36.

French, W. L., & Bell, C. H. (1999). *Organization development* (6th ed.). Upper Saddle River, NJ: Prentice-Hall.

Greenwald, B., & Kahn, J. (2005). *Competition demystified.* New York, NY: Penguin.

Griffith, S. B. (1963). *Sun Tzu: The art of war.* London, England: Oxford University Press.

Gulati, R., & Oldroyd, J. B. (2005). The quest for customer focus. *Harvard Business Review, 83,* 92–101.

Hamel, G. (1996). Strategy as revolution. *Harvard Business Review, 74,* 69–82.

Hamel, G., & Prahalad, C. K. (1992). Capabilities-based competition. *Harvard Business Review, 70,* 164–170.

Hamel, G., & Prahalad, C. K. (1994). *Competing for the future.* Boston, MA: Harvard Business School Press.

Hargadon, A. B., & Douglas, Y. (2001). When innovations meet institutions: Edison and the design of the electric light. *Administrative Science Quarterly, 46,* 476-501.

Harrington, R. J., Lemak, D. J., Reed, R., & Kendall, K. W. (2004). A question of fit: The links among environment, strategy formulation, and performance. *Journal of Business & Management, 10,* 15–38.

Hogan, J., Hogan, R., & Busch, C. M. (1984). How to measure service orientation. *Journal of Applied Psychology, 69,* 167–173.

Hooters Air Folds Its Wings. (2006, March 29). Aero News Network. Retrieved from http://www.aero-news.net/index.cfm?do=main.textpost&id=1b2004d8-a930-40ec-a1eb-8b25d7787d06

Hrebinaik, L. G., & Joyce, W. F. (2001). Implementing strategy: An appraisal and agenda for future research. In M. A. Hitt, R. E. Freeman, & J. S. Harrison (Eds.), *Handbook of strategic management* (pp. 602–626). Oxford, England: Blackwell.

Iacobucci, D. (1996). The quality improvement customers didn't want. *Harvard Business Review, 74,* 20–25.

Kaplan, R. S., & Norton, D. P. (2001). *The strategy-focused organization.* Boston, MA: Harvard Business School Press.

Kaplan, R. S., & Norton, D. P. (2004). *Strategy maps.* Boston, MA: Harvard Business School Press.

Khatri, N. (1994). *Strategic processes and organizational performance.* New York, NY: State University of New York.

Kim, W. C., & Mauborgne, R. (1999). Strategy, value innovation, and the knowledge economy. *Sloan Management Review, 40,* 41–54.

Kim, W. C., & Mauborgne, R. (2005). *Blue ocean strategy.* Boston, MA: Harvard Business School Press.

Lilly, P. (2011, November 5). Broadband blues: Millions of users still rocking AOL dial-up [Web log post]. Retrieved from http://hothardware.com/News/Broadband-Blues-Millions-of-Users-Still-Rocking-AOL-DialUp/

Loveman, G. (2003). Diamonds in the data mine. *Harvard Business Review, 81,* 109–113.

Maitlis, S. (2005). The social processes of organizational sensemaking. *Academy of Management Journal, 48,* 21–49.

McCarty, D. & Jinks, B. (2012, January 19). Kodak files for bankruptcy as digital era spells end to film. *Bloomberg.* Retrieved from http://www.bloomberg.com/news/2012-01-19/kodak-photography-pioneer-files-for-bankruptcy-protection-1-.html

McDonald, I., & Admay, J. (2006, January 13). Whole foods fare's pricey? Check out shares. *Wall Street Journal.*

Mintzberg, H. (1987). Crafting strategy. *Harvard Business Review, 65,* 66–75.

Mintzberg, H. (1994). *The rise and fall of strategic planning.* Boston, MA: Harvard Business School Press.

Panayides, P. M. (2004). Logistics service providers: an empirical study of marketing strategies and company performance. *International Journal of Logistics: Research & Applications, 7,* 1–15.

Payne, A., & Frow, P. (1999). Developing a segmented service strategy: Improving measurement in relationship marketing. *Journal of Marketing Management, 15,* 797–818.

Pophan, W. J., & Sirotnik, K. A. (1992). *Understanding statistics in education.* Itasca, IL: F. E. Peacock.

Porter, M. E. (1980). *Competitive strategy.* New York, NY: The Free Press.

Porter, M. E. (1996). What is strategy? *Harvard Business Review, 74,* 61–78.

Porter, M. E. (1998). Clusters and the new economics of competition. *Harvard Business Review, 76,* 77-90.

Porter, M. E. (2001). Strategy and the internet. *Harvard Business Review, 79,* 62–78.

Prokesch, S. E. (1995). Competing on customer service: An interview with British Airways' Sir Colin Marshall. *Harvard Business Review, 73,* 100–112.

Ramanujam, V., Venkatraman, N., & Camillus, J. C. (1986). Multi-objective assessment of effectiveness of strategic planning: A discriminant analysis approach. *Academy of Management Journal, 29,* 347–372.

Reinartz, W., & Kumar, V. (2002). The mismanagement of customer loyalty. *Harvard Business Review, 80,* 86–94.

Sacks, D. (2009, April 1). Lululemon's cult of selling. *Fast Company.* Retrieved from http://www.fastcompany.com/magazine/134/ommy.html

Schein, E. H. (2003). *DEC is dead, long live DEC.* San Francisco, CA: Berrett-Koehler.

Scheraga, D. (2004). What makes Wal-Mart tick. *Chain Store Age, 80,* 49–50.

Senge, P. M. (2006). *The fifth discipline.* New York, NY: Currency Doubleday.

Senge, P.M., Kleinger, A., Roberts. C., Ross, R., Roth, G., & Smith, B. (1999). *The dance of change: The challenges to sustaining momentum in learning organizations.* New York, NY: Currency Doubleday.

Stalk, G., Evans, P., & Shulman, L. E. (1992). Competing on capabilities: The new rules of corporate strategy. *Harvard Business Review, 70,* 54–66.

Strauss, A., & Corbin, J. (1998). *Basics of qualitative research* (2nd ed.). Thousand Oaks, CA: Sage.

Stych, E. (2012, February 14). Feds: Delta air lines' customer service improved in 2011. *Minneapolis St. Paul Business Journal.* Retrieved from http://www.bizjournals.com/twincities/news/2012/02/14/delta-customer-service-improves.html

Sutton, D., & Klein, T. (2003). *Enterprise marketing management.* Hoboken, NJ: Wiley.

Thomas, J. B., Clark, S. M., & Giola, D. A. (1993). Strategic sensemaking and organizational performance: Linkages among scanning, interpretation, action, and outcomes. *Academy of Management Journal, 36,* 239–270.

Ulrich, D., & Smallwood, N. (2004). Capitalizing on capabilities. *Harvard Business Review, 82,* 119–127.

Viguerie, S. P., & Thompson, C. (2005). The faster they fall. *Harvard Business Review, 83,* 22.

Waaser, E., Dahneke, M., Pekkarinen, M., & Weissel, M. (2004). How you slice it: Smarter segmentation for your sales force. *Harvard Business Review, 82,* 105–111.

Watson, A., & Wooldridge, B. (2005). Business unit manager influence on corporate-level strategy formulation. *Journal of Managerial Issues, 17,* 147–161.

Weiser, C. R. (1995). Championing the customer. *Harvard Business Review, 73,* 113-116.

Worley, C. G., Hitchin, D. E., & Ross, W. R. (1996). *Integrated strategic change.* Reading, MA: Addison-Wesley.

About the Author

Jimmy Brown, PhD, is the Strategy Practice Area Lead at Beacon Associates, where he is responsible for change management, organizational assessment/effectiveness, performance improvement, and business strategy consulting engagements. Prior to joining Beacon, he held senior-level consulting positions at marquee firms such as Booz-Allen & Hamilton, Accenture, and Hewlett-Packard. Dr. Brown is a frequent author and speaker on the topics of business strategy and organizational change. He has presented at major conferences such as the American Society for Training and Development, and the Academy of Management. He is regularly sought out for his insights on how to apply cutting-edge theory to solve real-world challenges. Dr. Brown received his master's degree in industrial and organizational psychology from the University of Tulsa, and his PhD from Benedictine University's award-winning organizational development program. In addition to his consulting work, he is a professor in several graduate psychology and management programs. He can be contacted at www.jimmybrownphd.com.